Commendations for *The Story of Scripture*

"It takes a courageous author to write an introduction to biblical theology, and Matt Emerson has written a careful and compelling work. *The Story of Scripture* is thoroughly biblical and immensely helpful, showing how all the parts of the redemptive narrative point to Jesus. This work helps us see the striking beauty of the story of Scripture, and leads us to respond in worship of the Savior."

—*Matt Boswell, hymn writer; founder, Doxology and Theology; and pastor of ministries and worship, Providence Church, Frisco, TX*

"I believe it's a sign of spiritual health that so many evangelicals have become interested in biblical theology. You hold in your hand (or see on your screen!) the best brief introduction to the discipline. In *The Story of Scripture*, Matt Emerson expertly translates technical concepts for general readers and thoughtfully applies biblical theology to life and ministry. The result is an indispensable resource and an excellent first entry in a promising series that will do much to equip pastors, strengthen churches, and advance Christ's kingdom."

—*Nathan A. Finn, dean of the School of Theology and Missions and professor of Christian thought and tradition, Union University*

"*The Story of Scripture* provides a robust perspective that speaks to the coherency and the unity of God's redemptive narrative. This book vigorously testifies to the person and work of Jesus Christ as the central theme of the Bible in a way that is informative and encouraging. Matthew Emerson has given us a resource that will serve both the pulpit and the pew well. It is with great enthusiasm that I recommend this work."

—*Earon M. James Sr., lead teaching pastor, Relevant Life Church, Pace, FL*

"If you have any interest in the Bible, then I encourage you to take up and read this little book! Many people know stories in the Bible, but they don't know the story of the Bible. Emerson has provided an easy-to-read introduction of biblical theology, showing the marvelous unity of the Bible, of which Jesus is the hero. *The Story of Scripture* will help you understand the redemptive drama of Scripture better, and will also build your faith, as you consider the divine nature of Scripture. I will be using it for years to come."

—*Tony Merida, associate professor of preaching, Southeastern Baptist Theological Seminary, and pastor for preaching and vision, Imago Dei Church, Raleigh, NC*

"If you are looking for a primer that combines a predictable evangelical high view of scripture with an unpredictable historic/Christocentric read of the Bible, you are holding it in your hand. Emerson has provided a faithful and helpful volume: broad enough in scope to grasp some of the principal points of biblical interpretation, yet readable enough for the curious beginner."

—*D. Jeffrey Mooney, professor of Old Testament interpretation and theology, California Baptist University, and senior pastor, Redeemer Baptist Church, Riverside, CA*

"This first volume of the promising Hobbs College Library is an insightful, solid, faithful, and edifying introduction to the biblical story and biblical theology. It will strengthen pastors, students, and church leaders alike."

—*Christopher W. Morgan, dean of the School of Christian Ministries and professor of theology, California Baptist University*

"*The Story of Scripture* masterfully demonstrates the continuity in the storyline of the Bible. Matthew Emerson offers a vivid, yet accessible, description of how biblical theology has been conducted throughout the course of church history, and traces the essential theme of redemption through the biblical narrative. The volume culminates with an invitation to participate in God's story, which it masterfully tells."

—*Walter R. Strickland II, associate vice president for kingdom diversity and assistant professor of systematic and contextual theology, Southeastern Baptist Theological Seminary*

"Matt Emerson's *The Story of Scripture* maps the theological unity of Scripture. The terrain of Scripture is presented through an insightful, close reading of the Bible. Emerson contributes to one's understanding of the biblical storyline by connecting how many sub-plots of the story connect to its main plot. He also adds brief, perceptive explanations of the underlying theological themes that construct the contours of the Bible. Emerson believes knowing how to apply biblical truth to our lives depends on recognizing the biblical story and where one is in the story. He persuasively illustrates this in his discussion on preaching, doctrine, biblical counseling, the Christian life, and the church's mission."

—*Keith S. Whitfield, dean of graduate studies, vice president for academic administration, and assistant professor of theology, Southeastern Baptist Theological Seminary*

Commendations for Hobbs College Library

"This series honors a wonderful servant of Christ with a stellar lineup of contributors. What a gift to the body of Christ! My hope and prayer is that it will be widely read and used for the glory of God and the good of his Church."

—*Daniel L. Akin, president, Southeastern Baptist Theological Seminary*

"This series is a must have, go-to resource for everyone who is serious about Bible study, teaching, and preaching. The authors are committed to the authority of the Bible and the vitality of the local church. I am excited about the kingdom impact of this much needed resource."

—*Hance Dilbeck, senior pastor, Quail Springs Baptist Church, Oklahoma City, OK*

"I am very excited about the dynamic leadership of Dr. Heath Thomas and his vision of the Hobbs College Library at Oklahoma Baptist University that he is developing. Through his work as Dean of the Hobbs College of Theology, this 21-volume set of books will ascend the theological understanding of laypeople, church leaders, pastors, and bi-vocational pastors. Therefore, I want to encourage you to participate in this vision that will equip your church to make a greater difference for Jesus Christ in your community and around the world."

—*Ronnie Floyd, senior pastor, Cross Church, Northwest AR, and former president, the Southern Baptist Convention*

"This series offers an outstanding opportunity for leaders of all kind to strengthen their knowledge of God, his word, and the manner in which we should engage the culture around us. Do not miss this opportunity to grow as a disciple of Jesus and as a leader of his church."

—*Micah Fries, senior pastor, Brainerd Baptist Church, Chattanooga, TN*

"The Hobbs College Library is a perfect way to help people who want to grow in the basics of their faith. Whether you are a layperson or longtime pastor, this tool will help give you the theological base needed for ministry today. I highly recommend this tremendous resource to anyone wanting to deepen their understanding of Scripture."

—*Jack Graham, pastor, Prestonwood Baptist Church, North TX, and former president, the Southern Baptist Convention*

"The best resources are those that develop the church theologically while instructing her practically in the work of the Great Commission. Dr. Thomas has assembled an impressive host of contributors for a new set of resources that will equip leaders at all levels who want to leave a lasting impact for the gospel. Dr. Hobbs exemplified the pastor-leader-theologian, and it's inspiring to see a series put out in his name that so aptly embodies his ministry and calling."

—*J.D. Greear, pastor, The Summit Church, Raleigh-Durham, NC*

"Unfortunately many of the church's most insightful resources aren't very accessible to the lay reader. That's why I'm excited about a series like the Hobbs College Library, where those of us without a PhD in a particular field are able to find wise guides who can show us biblical, theological, ethical, and ministerial truths that transform."

—*Jason Hood, director of advanced urban ministerial education, Gordon-Conwell Theological Seminary, Boston, MA*

"The Hobbs College Library is a favorable tool for the accomplishing of Ephesians 4:12-14 in the local church. With its diversity of scholarly contributions, leaders who introduce it to their laity can witness their people flourish in their walk with Christ as they live on mission for his glory."

—*D. A. Horton, pastor, Reach Fellowship, North Long Beach, CA, and chief evangelist, Urban Youth Workers Institute*

"For years, theological education has suffered from a failure to educate the layperson, young adults, and the busy, bi-vocational pastor. Theological training in the local church has been woefully abandoned, or watered-down, so that it tends to be too light; whereas, theological education in the seminary tends to be too heavy and involved for most of these Christians to pursue. So, I'm thrilled to recommend this series of books that hits this massive middle! Trusted pastors and leaders have provided the church with gold here. May God use it to equip and bless Christ's church for years to come!"

—*Tony Merida, pastor for preaching and vision, Imago Dei Church, Raleigh, NC, and associate professor of preaching, Southeastern Baptist Theological Seminary.*

THE STORY
OF SCRIPTURE

THE STORY
OF SCRIPTURE

*An Introduction
to Biblical Theology*

MATTHEW Y. EMERSON

HEATH A. THOMAS, *Editor*

OBU

ACADEMIC

NASHVILLE, TENNESSEE

The Story of Scripture: An Introduction to Biblical Theology
Copyright © 2017 by Matthew Y. Emerson
Published by B&H Academic
Nashville, Tennessee

ISBN: 978-1-4627-5875-3

Dewey Decimal Classification: 220.1
Subject Heading: BIBLE--HISTORY \ BIBLE--INSPIRATION \
JESUS CHRIST

Printed in the United States of America
1 2 3 4 5 6 7 8 9 10 • 22 21 20 19 18 17

To Abigail, the joy of my heart;

and to Madelyn and Sophia, a double portion

of God's kindness toward me.

Contents

Acknowledgments

While I take the sole blame for any deficiencies in what follows, many have contributed to what is commendable in this book, and to whom I owe my thanks. First, I wrote this book at the invitation of my dean and friend, Heath Thomas, who also serves as the editor of the Hobbs College Library. Heath has been instrumental in my growth as a reader of Scripture over the past decade, and he continued to offer his invaluable time and counsel during this project. This book is better because of his friendship and editorial oversight. I would also like to thank the editorial team at B&H Academic, and especially Chris Thompson for his direction in not only this volume but also the entire Hobbs College Library. Special thanks are due to my wife, Alicia, and five daughters; I wrote this book in the summer of 2016, while the older two were home from school and while Abigail and our (now two-year-old) twin girls, Madelyn and Sophia, required abundant amounts of attention. Alicia, I could not do anything I have done without your support and encouragement.

And I am eternally and fundamentally grateful to our Triune God, without whom I would still be blind to the truths of Scripture and deaf to its call to repent and believe in the incarnate, cruci-fied-and-resurrected Son of God. I would be wandering in a story of my own making, a story without meaning and point. Instead, be-cause of the graciousness of God in Christ, I am by the power of his Spirit finding my place in his story, the story of the world that finds its center in the person and work of Jesus.

About the Library

The Hobbs College Library equips Christians with tools for growing in the faith and for effective ministry. The library trains its readers in three major areas: Bible, theology, and ministry. The series originates from the Herschel H. Hobbs College of Theology and Ministry at Oklahoma Baptist University, where biblical, orthodox, and practical education lies at its core. Training the next generation was important for the great Baptist statesman Dr. Herschel H. Hobbs, and the Hobbs College that bears his name fosters that same vision.

The Hobbs College Library: Biblical. Orthodox. Practical.

CHAPTER 1

Introduction: What Is Biblical Theology?

*"The Bible contains sixty-six books written by
more than forty authors, but is ultimately one book
written by one author—God the Holy Spirit."*

This axiom, which you may have heard, is undoubtedly true. The
Bible is one book written by one divine author, but God used
many different human authors to do the writing. But when we ask
how exactly the Bible fits together as one book, our agreement may
begin to unravel. Is the Bible one book only because the Holy Spirit
authored it all? Or is there some other way that it coheres together as
one book? People have answered these questions differently through
the centuries.

Biblical Theology and the Question of Unity

This question—how is the Bible one book?—is often answered
through the tools of biblical theology. As a discipline, biblical theology exists to explain the unity and distinctions between the biblical

books. Over the past three centuries, biblical scholars have answered the question in a variety of ways. To get an understanding of how the Bible coheres as a unified book, let's look at a few ways people have understood "biblical theology."

Johannes Gabler's Project: Historical Development

The "father of biblical theology," Johannes P. Gabler, saw biblical theology as primarily *an historical task*. In his address to the University of Altdorff in 1787, Gabler made a distinction between biblical theology, inquiry concerned with the historical setting and religious function of particular biblical books and authors, and dogmatic theology, an ecclesial enterprise focused on the impact of the Bible on its contemporary readers.[1]

For Gabler and those who followed him, particularly William Wrede, biblical theology is a purely historical, descriptive task— "what it meant"—while dogmatic, or systematic, theology is a constructive, prescriptive task—"what it means."[2] The former is done in the academy, the latter in the church. The former tends to be willing to depart from traditional Christian beliefs, while the latter is focused on reading the Bible in the context of the church's historic confessions.

---

[1] Johannes P. Gabler, "An Oration on the Proper Distinction Between Biblical and Dogmatic Theology and the Specific Objectives of Each," in *Old Testament Theology: Flowering and Future,* Sources for Biblical and Theological Study, *ed.* Ben C. Ollenburger (Winona Lake, IN: Eisenbrauns, 2004).

[2] For an introduction to William Wrede's thought, as well as to that of his contemporary opponent Adolf Schlatter, see Robert W. Morgan, *The Nature of New Testament Theology: The Contribution of William Wrede and Adolf Schlatter*, SBT 2.25 (Eugene, OR: Wipf and Stock, 2009). On the distinction between "what it meant" and "what it means" and particularly its use by Krister Stendahl, see the summary in Edward W. Klink and Darian R. Lockett, *Understanding Biblical Theology: A Comparison of Theory and Practice* (Grand Rapids: Zondervan, 2012), 29–33.

In Gabler's model, then, biblical theology is an attempt to describe the religious beliefs of biblical authors and communities at the time a particular biblical book was written. Any unity between books or between the two testaments exists as a historical unity, one that arises because of historical continuity between religious communities. Unity is not a product of the continuity provided by divine inspiration of each biblical author, nor of a similar subject shared by each biblical author. Rather, unity is solely the product of one biblical author being historically situated in the same religious and theological stream as another biblical author. For many biblical theologians that follow Gabler, then, different streams and trajectories are within the Bible, some of which contradict one another.

Let me provide two examples of how this approach to biblical theology works out in practice. Among New Testament theologians it is popular to assert that a difference exists between the charismatic, imminent eschatological expectation of "authentically Pauline" letters like 1 Corinthians and the more settled, delayed eschatological expectation of "deutero-Pauline" letters such as 1 Timothy. Another example some give is the supposed contradiction between James's soteriology and Paul's soteriology in Romans. Now let me be clear: I do not find either of these conclusions to be justified! Still, this is one way this form of biblical theology works itself out. To be fair, I need to say this approach does not always end up with contradiction or discord. That would be to say too much because scholars such as Balla follow Gabler and Wrede's approach but do not find disunity in the biblical material.[3] Nevertheless, any unity

---

[3] For example, Peter Balla attempts a New Testament theology using Gabler and Wrede's approach but does so in such a way that he sees historical unity between the books of the New Testament. See his *Challenges to New Testament Theology:*

they find is historically situated and not explicitly tied to the nature of Scripture or its authorship.

Geerhardus Vos: Conceptual and Structural Unity

A second model of biblical theology pays attention to the divine authorship of Scripture and assumes a theological unity based on that fact. This model, typically traced to Geerhardus Vos,[4] sees the two testaments tied together based on:

1. Scripture's Subject: Jesus Christ
2. Scripture's Story: the grand narrative from creation (Genesis 1) to new creation (Revelation 21)

While there are different articulations of this model and ways of demonstrating this unity, each of them share a recognition that the Bible is ultimately one coherent story, usually described as Creation-Fall-Redemption, that points to and culminates in the person and work of Jesus, the Son.

Developing from this overall structure Vos pioneered, there are at least three schools of thought on how this story fits together and how individual passages point to Christ, helpfully summarized by Klink and Lockett:[5]

1. The so-called *Dallas school* seeks to situate a passage in its historical context and ask what it says to Israel or the church

---

An Attempt to Justify the Enterprise, WUNT 2, Reihe 95 (Tübingen: Mohr Siebeck, 1997; repr., Grand Rapids: Baker Academic, 2011).

[4] See Geerhardus Vos, *Biblical Theology: Old and New Testaments* (Grand Rapids: Eerdmans, 1948; repr., Carlisle, PA: Banner of Truth Trust, 1975, 2012).

[5] See Klink and Lockett, *Understanding Biblical Theology*, 59–75.

at that moment. While there is a recognition that the passage fits into the larger biblical story, there is reticence in this school to import any later developments of the passage into its original message.

2. The *Chicago school* also seeks to situate a passage in its historical context, but here there is also a willingness to see how the passage develops and furthers the biblical narrative. So, for instance, in Gen 3:15, the Chicago school would ask what the passage's original readers would have understood by it, as would the Dallas school. Rather than stopping there, as the Dallas school would, the Chicago school asks how that passage develops and is fulfilled in the rest of the biblical story. There is a willingness to see how the text moves the biblical narrative forward.

3. The *Philadelphia school* asks not only about the passage's historical context but also its literary context. It wants to know everything the Dallas and Chicago school does, but it also asks (a) how the passage itself points to Christ and (b) how its canonical context informs the interpretation of the passage. In other words, while the Dallas school and Chicago school would be reticent to say that Gen 3:15 "is about" Jesus, the Philadelphia school would be willing to import the canonical development of the passage back into its message. In any case, each of these three approaches seeks to discern how a passage fits into not only its historical context but also its canonical literary context. In other words, they ask the question, "How does this passage fit into the big story of the whole Bible?" And, in the case of the Philadelphia school, a second question augments the first: "How does this passage point to the culmination of the biblical story, the person and work of Jesus Christ?"

From the section above, we can see how scholars have understood biblical theology and the unity of Scripture in the past 250 years or so. But what about in the early church? What about from the time before Gabler? When we look at that time period, we gain insight on the church's view of biblical theology and Scriptural unity. The early church helps us to ask biblical theological questions related to the subject and structure of Scripture. And key to our understanding is the figure of Irenaeus, the bishop of Lyons.

Biblical Theology and the Early Church

Irenaeus, a second-century apologist and theologian, argued that we should read the Bible with at least three things in mind.[6] First, we ought to read Scripture with its *hypothesis* in view. Irenaeus used this term to indicate there is a main idea—the person and work of Jesus Christ—to which each passage in the Bible points. To help his readers understand this term, Irenaeus employed the analogy of a mosaic—a portrait made of different pieces of stained glass. For us today the corresponding analogy might be of a puzzle. In both a mosaic and a puzzle, the many pieces could be put together in any number of ways. Only when we have access to the plan for the mosaic, or the puzzle box top, do we know how to put the pieces together properly.

For Irenaeus, the mosaic pieces are supposed to be put together in such a way that they show readers of Scripture the handsome King, Jesus Christ. To put it in puzzle terms, the box top shows us that the pieces fit together to form a picture of Jesus. As we read

---

[6] On Irenaeus's interpretive method and these three terms, see John O'Keefe and R. R. Reno, *Sanctified Vision: An Introduction to Early Christian Interpretation of the Bible* (Baltimore: The Johns Hopkins University Press, 2005), 34–44.

with the hypothesis in mind, then, our goal is always to find how a particular puzzle piece, or scriptural passage, fits into the larger puzzle that shows us Jesus Christ.

Irenaeus employed two other tools to assist in seeing how particular passages point to Christ. The first, *economy*, seeks to understand how a text fits into the structure of the Bible. Particularly important for Irenaeus is the recognition of the shape of the biblical story, a shape that culminates in the incarnation, life, death, resurrection, and ascension of the God-Man, Jesus Christ. Much like Vos almost two millennia later, Irenaeus asks how particular texts of Scripture fit into the larger story of the Bible, and especially how those texts point forward or backward to Scripture's climax found in the life and work of Jesus of Nazareth.

In seeking to understand how texts fit into the grand narrative of Scripture, Irenaeus employed a final hermeneutical tool, what he called *recapitulation*. For Irenaeus, each story in the Bible finds its culmination in the person and work of Jesus Christ, not only in terms of historical progression but in terms of typology. For instance, while the story of Abram and Sarai progresses the biblical narrative in terms of the covenant God makes with them and the line of the seed continuing through Isaac, both of which ultimately progress to the person and work of Jesus, it is not merely their place in the history of redemption that points to Jesus. For Irenaeus, the actual details of each biblical story are patterned after and point to the one main story, the story of Jesus in the Gospels. As an example, Sarai's barrenness and miraculous conception point forward to both Elizabeth's barrenness and miraculous conception of John the Baptist and to Mary's miraculous conception of Jesus.

Biblical Theology and the Bible's Unity

While current practitioners in the stream of Vos's biblical theology may not agree with every tool Irenaeus uses, the conclusions he makes, or even the manner in which he describes either his tools or his conclusions, there are affinities between this early church interpreter and today's biblical theologians.

For example, G. K. Beale emphasizes the story of the Bible, seeing how each passage fits into that story, intertextuality (how certain texts quote or allude to previous texts), and how a particular passage in the Old Testament may both historically and conceptually progress toward the person and work of Jesus.[7] Beale refers to his method as organic, in that Old Testament texts are like seeds that flower out. As we read these Old Testament texts, we follow their progression through other, later Old Testament passages that all eventually find their culmination and fulfillment in Jesus Christ.

Likewise, biblical theologians like Peter Leithart[8] and Scott Hahn[9] see an abundance of narrative patterns—what Irenaeus called recapitulation and what we commonly refer to as typology—that find their culmination and fulfillment in Israel's Messiah. So, while Irenaeus's terms may not be used with much frequency today, and while there is variety within Vos's stream of biblical theology, again we can say that what holds this approach together is an attempt to read each passage and book of Scripture within its larger narrative

---

[7] For a fuller articulation of this method, see G. K. Beale, *A New Testament Biblical Theology: The Unfolding of the Old Testament in the New* (Grand Rapids: Baker Academic, 2011), 1–29.

[8] See, for example, Peter Leithart, *A Son to Me: An Exposition of 1 & 2 Samuel* (Moscow, ID: Canon, 2003).

[9] See Scott Hahn, *The Kingdom of God as Liturgical Empire: A Theological Commentary on 1 & 2 Chronicles* (Grand Rapids: Baker Academic, 2012).

context and as pointing to the climax of the biblical story, Jesus Christ:

- The unity of the Bible is found in its structure—the grand narrative of Scripture—and its subject—the incarnate Christ.
- This unity is grounded in what the Bible is. It is the Spirit-inspired, Son-centered, Father-revealing Word of God.

The Bible's Theological Unity

In other words, the Bible is ultimately one book given by one author for one purpose. The Bible is a trinitarian book. Scripture is given by the Father to reveal the Son by the power of the Spirit. In this way, it is "trinitarian." God has given Scripture to his people in the context of the covenant of salvation he has made with them. God gives Scripture to us so we might know him. The Bible is written to reveal the God of the universe to us. Its purpose is to make the one God, Yahweh, known to his people, his people who have been redeemed through his covenant-keeping work.

When we think about the Bible, then, we need to come to it understanding the context in which it is given and the purpose for which it is given. The Spirit inspires Scripture in the context of God's work of salvation, and he does so in order that his people might know how to come to him and know him fully. The Bible is not just an instruction manual, although it certainly gives instructions; it is not just a guide for moral living, although it certainly addresses morality; and it is not just an anthology of disparate stories, only connected by the front and back cover. The Bible is a covenant book, given to God's covenant people so they might know him fully.

The Bible's Trinitarian Shape

The triune God makes himself known specifically through the person of God the Son. Therefore, the Bible is not only about God generally, or about the Father in some places, the Son in some places, and the Spirit in some places. Instead, God chooses to reveal himself particularly through the person of the Son.[10] This has to do with how the Trinity works in creation and redemption. God the Father works and is known through God the Son, who works and is known by God the Holy Spirit. When we think about the Bible, then, we need to think about it along the lines of the trinitarian God.

If God gives us the Bible to make himself known to us, how does he accomplish that as one God in three persons? We begin by acknowledging that God the Holy Spirit inspires Scripture (2 Tim 3:16–17). But he inspires it to what end? Jesus tells us that the Spirit's role in revelation is to testify to the Son (John 17:14; 2 Cor 3:17–18). As the Spirit inspires the writers of Scripture, then, he is continually pointing toward the Son, and particularly to the person and work of the incarnate Son, Jesus of Nazareth. We can and should, therefore, say that the entire Bible points to Christ (cf. Luke 16:29–31; 24:27,44; John 5:39,46). And the reason that this is so, the reason that the Spirit testifies to the Son, is it is through seeing and knowing the Son that we see and know the Father. "He who has seen me has seen the Father," says Jesus (John 14:9; also 12:45; cf. 6:45–46; 8:19; 14:7). Further, the writer of Hebrews tells us the ultimate revelation of the Father comes through the Son (1:2), who

---

[10] On the trinitarian shape of Scripture, both in terms of its narrative Christological climax and its Christocentric revelation of the triune God, see Scott R. Swain, *Trinity, Revelation, and Reading: A Theological Introduction to the Bible and its Interpretation* (London: T&T Clark, 2011), esp. 15–60.

is "the radiance of the glory of God and the exact imprint of his nature" (1:3 ESV). If we want to see the Father, we look at the Son. Because we cannot see Jesus face to face until we meet him either in paradise or at his return, we must know him through that which testifies to him—the Bible.

Therefore, we know the Son through the Scriptures, which the Spirit inspired. To say that the Bible is about God is to say that it testifies to the Son by the Spirit so that we might know and see the Father. Saying that the Bible is about Jesus is not to say that it is *only* about Jesus and not about the Father or Spirit, but to say that we know the Father through knowing the Son, whom we know through the Scriptures inspired by the Spirit.[11]

One Subject and One Story

This brings us back to the two aspects of Scripture that unite the Bible's sixty-six books into one book—its subject matter and its structure. The subject matter is Jesus, and we see how passages point to Jesus through understanding their place in the structure of Scripture. The next two chapters will articulate the broad structure of the Bible, or the grand narrative of Scripture, but for now we can summarize it as Creation, Fall, Redemption, Restoration (or New Creation).[12] The Bible begins with God's creation of the world and

---

[11] On this trinitarian unity via Christological focus, see also Graeme Goldsworthy, *According to Plan: An Introduction to Biblical Theology* (Downers Grove, IL: IVP Academic, 1991), 29–80.

[12] On this outline, see, for example, Craig G. Bartholomew and Michael W. Goheen, *The Drama of Scripture: Finding Our Place in the Biblical Story* (Grand Rapids: Baker Academic, 2004); Tim Chester, *From Creation to New Creation: Making Sense of the Whole Bible Story*, 2nd ed. (Purcellville, VA: The Good Book Company,

its fall into sin through Adam and Eve, and then the rest of Scripture is taken up with the story of God's plan to redeem the cosmos. Situating a particular passage within this big picture is vital to biblical theology and biblical interpretation.

In addition to this narrative context, a number of concepts will assist us in seeing how and why structure is important to biblical theology. We begin with *recapitulation*, a word we have already seen in this chapter. Commonly known as *typology*,[13] recapitulation demonstrates a structural unity to the Bible and its story through patterns of smaller stories. These repetitive, smaller stories build up and point to the climax of the one big story of the Bible, the person and work of Jesus. So, for instance, the Joseph story is repeated throughout the Old Testament, particularly in the stories of Mordecai and Daniel.[14] Like Joseph, Mordecai and Daniel flee from sin, are exiled in Gentile kingdoms, and rise to second in command of those kingdoms. Mordecai, like Joseph, is clothed in the image of the king and is paraded through the capital city; Daniel, like Joseph, is able to interpret dreams. Joseph, in turn, is pictured as a new Adam: one who is clothed in the image of the king; is second in command to the king; rules over the land given by the king; is given a wife by the king; is fruitful and multiplies; and, unlike Adam, is

2010); Goldsworthy, *According to Plan*, 80–236; and Vaughn Roberts, *God's Big Picture: Tracing the Storyline of the Bible* (Downers Grove, IL: IVP, 2003).

[13] For an introduction to typology, see Francis Foulkes, "The Acts of God: A Study of the Basis of Typology in the Old Testament," in *The Right Doctrine from the Wrong Texts? Essays on the Use of the Old Testament in the New*, ed. G. K. Beale (Grand Rapids: Baker, 1994), 342–74; and Graeme Goldsworthy, *Christ-Centered Biblical Theology: Hermeneutical Foundations and Principles* (Downers Grove, IL: IVP Academic, 2012), 170–89.

[14] I owe this insight, along with many others, to Dr. Robert L. Cole, formerly associate professor of Old Testament and Semitics at Southeastern Baptist Theological Seminary (SEBTS) in Wake Forest, NC.

wise, discerning between good and evil. There is a repeated pattern, in other words, from Adam to Joseph to Daniel to Mordecai. This repeated pattern, in turn, points to and finds its culmination in the coming Messiah, Jesus, who is the image of God, the exact representation of his being (Heb 1:3; i.e., Jesus is *clothed* in the image of God), able to discern between good and evil (Matthew 4), fruitful and multiplies through his Spirit in the Church's testimony (Acts 1:8), and rules over all things (Eph 1:20; Col 1:15–17). Jesus, the Second Adam, is the culmination of the pattern of the First Adam found in the Old Testament.

Related to this repetition of stories with the Bible is another key concept, *intertextuality*.[15] This term refers to passages that quote or allude to previous passages of Scripture. In the example of typology above, not only do the patterns of the stories match, but the authors of those different books quote or allude to the similar stories in previous books. So, Mordecai's story looks like Joseph's story, but the author of Esther goes beyond narrative parallels and actually quotes from Genesis 37–50. Likewise, the Joseph story quotes and alludes back to Genesis 1–2 in portraying Joseph like a new Adam. This kind of textual unity occurs throughout the Bible, in both testaments. The human authors of Scripture were inspired by the divine Author to connect their books to other books of the Bible on a textual level. We should, therefore, pay attention to how particular verses repeat or allude to other verses of Scripture. Further, we should pay attention to how these textual connections help us to see the Bible's structural and conceptual unity. Many times these intertextual connections are related to one or both of those. So, for instance, the

---

[15] For an introduction to the concept of intertextuality, see John H. Sailhamer, *Introduction to Old Testament Theology: A Canonical Approach* (Grand Rapids: Zondervan, 1995), 212–13.

parallels between Adam and Joseph, and then between Joseph and Daniel and Mordecai, help us to see the typological, structural unity of those stories, which in turn points us to Scripture's conceptual unity in that all of them point forward to Jesus.

A fourth important concept that helps us to see the Bible's structural unity is that of *covenant*.[16] The whole Bible is tied together through the covenants God makes with his people. The one covenant of salvation God makes progresses throughout the Old Testament and culminates with the new covenant inaugurated by Jesus. So, after humanity's fall into sin:

1. God makes a covenant with Adam to crush Satan through the seed of woman.
2. He then makes a covenant with Noah not to destroy the earth before that redemption is accomplished (Genesis 6–9).
3. Next, he makes a covenant with Abram to bring the Messiah through his line and to make Abram a great nation (Israel) (Genesis 12; 15; 17; and 22).
4. After the Exodus, he makes a covenant with Israel regarding the land and the law (Exodus 19–23).
5. During David's reign, God promises him that David's son will sit on his throne forever and that he will build God's house (2 Samuel 7).
5. And through the prophets God promises that, in the new covenant, Israel, exiled and scattered, will one day be restored and receive God's Spirit so that they can follow God's instruction and live under his reign, forever (Jeremiah 31–33).

---

[16] On the Bible's covenantal structure, see Peter J. Gentry and Stephen J. Wellum, *Kingdom through Covenant: A Biblical-Theological Understanding of the Covenants* (Wheaton, IL: Crossway, 2012).

We will discuss the unity of these covenants, and the unique conditional nature of the Mosaic covenant, in a later chapter. For now, we simply want to note that these covenants tie the different parts of the Old Testament together and progress the entire Old Testament toward their fulfillment in Christ.

Finally, in addition to these narrative, textual, covenantal, and typological connective tissues, the Old and New Testament canons are structured in such a way that points to the Bible's unity. When we think about the Old Testament's structure, and particularly the order of the books in it, our English Bibles put the prophets at the end. This certainly helps us to see that the entire Old Testament ultimately points to Christ—it ends with prophetic hope about the coming Messiah.

But the order of the books in the Hebrew Bible, which differs significantly from our English Bibles, demonstrates an eschatological messianic hope as well.[17] In the Hebrew Bible, the Law (Genesis–Deuteronomy) comes first, followed by the Prophets, both Former (Joshua, Judges, Samuel, Kings) and Latter (Isaiah, Jeremiah, Ezekiel, Hosea–Malachi). Finally, the Hebrew Bible ends with the Writings (Psalms, Job, Proverbs, Ruth, Song of Solomon, Ecclesiastes, Lamentations, Esther, Daniel, Ezra–Nehemiah, Chronicles). As you can see, this order differs significantly from our English order. But there are narrative, textual connections that help us to see this order as pointing forward to the Messiah as well. The most important of these is the fact that at end of the Law (Deuteronomy 34), the beginning and end of the Prophets (Joshua 1 and Malachi 4), and the beginning of the Writings (Psalm 1), there are intertextual

---

[17] For an introduction to the Bible's shape, see my *Christ and the New Creation: A Canonical Approach to the Theology of the New Testament* (Eugene, OR: Wipf and Stock, 2013).

connections that tie each of these three sections together.[18] These are typically referred to as "seams," and if you were to go read each of those passages, you'd notice that all four of them are looking for a prophet greater than Moses, a wise king who will lead God's people into the promised land. In other words, each of the three sections of the Hebrew Bible is waiting for the same person. It evokes the same eschatological messianic hope that our English order has by ending with the prophets.

Conclusion

It might be helpful to picture Scripture by using a few different metaphors. One is the puzzle metaphor Irenaeus discussed. Another might be to see the Bible as an intricate quilt. The different stories and passages are different patches on the quilt, while the intertextual links are the seams in between them. Further, this quilt is made in such a way that all these patches move on the quilt toward one central patch, the patch that shows us the incarnate Christ. Or, to put it like Irenaeus, the whole puzzle is a picture of Jesus. The different pieces are the different stories and passages of the biblical books. The lines that fit together are the textual and narrative links between them. Whatever metaphor we use, the point is the same: the whole Bible is one book inspired by one author with one story that culminates in one person, the God-Man Jesus Christ. Biblical theology is

---

[18] On the connection between Deuteronomy 34 and Malachi 4, see Stephen B. Chapman, *The Law and the Prophets: A Study in the Old Testament Canon Formation*, FAT 27, ed. Bernd Janowski and Herman Spieckermann (Tübingen: J. C. B. Mohr, 2000), 112. On all four seams mentioned and their textual connections, see Sailhamer, *Introduction to Old Testament Theology,* 101.

the attempt to read the Bible in this structurally and conceptually unified fashion.

For the purposes of this book, while we will come back to the metaphors of the quilt and the puzzle, the dominant metaphor on which I will rely is that of a topographical map. These kinds of maps show you the whole terrain—you can see where you are, where you are going, and what kind of routes you can take to get there. But it also shows you the individual regions, the smaller areas of the map that, put together, make up the larger whole. As well, biblical theology gives us both of these—the big picture of the whole Bible *and* how its individual parts fit into that larger whole. Michael Horton says it this way:

> Like a topographical map, biblical theology draws all of the strands together to help us see the organic development of revelation and redemption from election to glorification. We see the high peaks, low valleys, rivers, and plains that lead from promise to fulfillment. Biblical theology rivets our attention to the historical development of various themes . . . the "many times" and "many ways" in which "God spoke to our fathers by the prophets, but in these last days . . . by his Son" (Heb 1:1–2).[19]

---

[19] Michael Horton, *The Christian Faith: A Systematic Theology for Pilgrims on the Way* (Grand Rapids: Zondervan, 2011), 28. For this geographical and traveling analogy, also see Mark J. Boda, "Biblical Theology and Old Testament Interpretation," pp. 122–54 in *Hearing the Old Testament: Listening for God's Address*, ed. Craig G. Bartholomew and David J. H. Beldman (Grand Rapids: Eerdmans, 2012), 135–47.

Biblical theology, then, helps us to see the end goal of the biblical narrative—Jesus—as well as how its different parts fit into that one main Christological pathway of Scripture.

In the remainder of this book, we will walk through the basics of that kind of reading, first by telling the whole story of the Bible, from Creation to New Creation, and then by noting a number of key structural and thematic ties between the different parts of Scripture. Ultimately, our goal is to see how the Bible fits together as one book about one person, Jesus Christ, God the Son in human flesh.

CHAPTER 2

The Story of the Bible, Part 1

As we have discussed, the Bible is one book by one author with one story and one subject: Jesus. The goal of this chapter and the next is to articulate the story-shape of Scripture, commonly known as Creation, Fall, Redemption, Restoration (or New Creation).

Creation

As the name of that first piece of the storyline indicates, the story of the Bible begins with creation in Genesis 1–2. God makes all things—heaven and earth, the heavenly bodies, water, land, sky, plants, fish, birds, insects, and animals—in 1:1–25. God creates all things through his Word and Spirit, as seen in his Spirit hovering over the waters in 1:2 and in him speaking everything into existence in the rest of the chapter. While Moses did not have the nuanced view of the Trinity that arose in the fourth century AD, we do see in Genesis 1 God already working in trinitarian fashion—the Father creates through his Word and his Spirit.[1]

The pinnacle of God's creative work comes at the end of the sixth day when he makes human beings (1:26–28). These verses teach us that human beings uniquely bear the image of God in his created world. While there has historically been much debate over what the image of God is, given God's instructions to Adam and Eve and the historical context of the ancient Near East, we can say that the *imago dei* is functional and ontological.[2] That is, it indicates *why* God made humans and *what* humans are.

With respect to the latter, humans bearing the image of God means that they uniquely demonstrate to the world who God is and what he is like. It also means that they have a unique way of relating to God, through their spirit (or soul). We see this particularly in Genesis 2, when God creates Adam by first forming his body out of the dust of the ground and then breathing his spirit into him. Adam and Eve are, thus, both body and soul, body like the rest of creation but uniquely soul-ish in their image-bearing relationship to God. Human beings are, therefore, relational at their core, not only to one another or to the rest of the creation but to God, and they are pictures of who God is and what he is like.

With respect to why human beings exist, or their function, the fact that they bear God's image tells us they are his representatives in his creation. We see this in the language of image bearing itself, as this kind of terminology was used in the ancient Near East to

---

[1] On how Genesis 1 can be considered trinitarian even though written in an ancient Near Eastern context, see Francis Watson, *Text, Church, and World: Biblical Interpretation in Theological Perspective* (Grand Rapids: Eerdmans, 1994), 137–53.

[2] On the *imago dei,* see Anthony R. Hoekema, *Created in God's Image* (Grand Rapids: Eerdmans, 1986).

indicate that a certain person represented someone else, usually the king. An image bearer was therefore an ambassador, a representative of his ruler's authority.[3] For Adam and Eve to be image bearers means, then, they are God's representatives on earth, the wielders of his authority, his vice regents.[4]

We also see the functional aspect of image bearing in the tasks that God gives to Adam and Eve. First, he tells them to "be fruitful and multiply and fill all the earth" (1:28). This is not merely a command to have bunches of babies; rather, filling the earth with offspring means filling it with more image bearers.[5] God wants his entire creation to be filled with those who bear his image and wield his authority. Second, he tells them to exercise that derivative authority by not only filling the earth but also subduing it, and to "have dominion over the fish of the sea and over the birds of the heavens and over every living thing that moves on the earth" (1:28). Adam and Eve are not only supposed to fill the earth; they are also supposed to rule over the entire cosmos. "Dominion" and "subdue" sometimes have negative connotations in modern cultures, but God does not mean here that Adam and Eve are allowed to trash the

---

[3] See G. K. Beale, *The Temple and the Church's Mission: A Biblical Theology of the Dwelling Place of God*, NSBT (Grand Rapids: IVP, 2004), 66–70. For an overview, including footnotes for further research on the garden in its ancient Near Eastern context and its temple imagery, see T. Desmond Alexander, *From Eden to the New Jerusalem: An Introduction to Biblical Theology* (Grand Rapids: Kregel Academic, 2008), 20–27.

[4] William J. Dumbrell, *The Faith of Israel: A Theological Survey of the Old Testament*, 2nd ed. (Grand Rapids: Baker Academic, 2002), 17.

[5] Stephen G. Dempster, *Dominion and Dynasty: A Theology of the Hebrew Bible*, ed. D. A. Carson (Downers Grove, IL: InterVarsity, 2003), 61.

place. Rather, God wants Adam and Eve to exercise godly authority, caring authority over his creation.[6]

God's design for Adam and Eve to exercise godly, caring authority becomes clear in the third task that God gives Adam and Eve, to "cultivate and keep" the garden (2:15). God has given Adam and Eve a land in which to dwell and which they are to rule, but it is a fruitful land that provides food for them (1:29–31) and where God dwells with them. It is, thus, a land that is a blessing and for which they must provide care, both for their physical and spiritual nourishment.[7] They are also to rule and cultivate under God's direction, and so the fourth task God gives them as image bearers is to obey his law. He only gives them one law, to refrain from eating from the tree of the knowledge of good and evil (2:15–17), but it governs them entirely.

So, God made Adam and Eve to be fruitful and multiply and fill all the earth with other worshippers and image bearers of Yahweh, to rule over the land he gave them, to cultivate and keep the good land he gave them, and to obey his law he gave to govern them.[8]

Fall

Notoriously, Adam and Eve do not last long in this good state of things. The serpent creeps into the garden and tempts Adam and Eve

---

[6] Vaughn Roberts, *God's Big Picture: Tracing the Storyline of the Bible* (Downers Grove, IL: IVP, 2003), 31.

[7] The verbs "cultivate and keep" occur in the Levitical narratives about the priests taking care of the temple but are translated as "worship and obey." See Umberto Cassuto, *Commentary on Genesis*, vol. 1 (Jerusalem: Magnes, 1964), 122–23.

[8] On the covenantal nature of these tasks, see Michael D. Williams, *Far as the Curse Is Found: The Covenant Story of Redemption* (Phillipsburg, NJ: P&R, 2005), 48–52.

to eat from the forbidden tree. The enemy tempts Eve by questioning God's word—"did God really say . . . ?"—and God's love[9]—"God doesn't want you to be like him." Eve, in response, fails to listen—she twists God's word—and then fails to obey. Adam, complacent, eats when Eve offers the fruit to him. God then shows up, seeking his wayward children, who have hidden from him. When they show themselves, they emerge still hidden, in that they have covered up their nakedness. They do not want God or each other to see them as they truly are. God asks what happened, and Adam and Eve proceed to shift the blame. First Adam blames Eve, and then Eve blames the serpent.

In response, God issues a number of punishments. One crucial aspect to note about these punishments is that they correspond to the tasks that God gave to Adam and Eve in Genesis 1–2.[10] After cursing the serpent (to which we will return in a moment), God punishes Eve in two ways. He first tells her that, from now on, it will be painful to bear children. He then tells her that "her desire will be for her husband, but he shall rule over you." The word *desire* here is not a positive term; rather, it indicates a desire to master, rule, or oppress the husband. This desire will be thwarted, though, and in turn there will be strife between husband and wife. These two punishments both relate to the primary task God gave to Adam and Eve, to be fruitful and multiply. Not only will it hurt to have babies, but the tension between husband and wife will make it difficult to conceive babies as well.

God punishes Adam for his sins. First, he tells Adam that the ground is cursed because of him, and that it will be difficult to bring

---

[9] I owe this insight to Steven Wade, associate professor of Biblical Counseling at SEBTS. Whether or not he gleaned it from another source, I do not know.

[10] Dumbrell, *The Faith of Israel,* 22–23.

forth sustenance from the ground. Instead of all the green plants available to him and his wife in Gen 1:29–31, the ground will bring forth thorns and thistles when Adam works it. Instead of food being easily available, Adam will have to toil by the sweat of his brow to make anything grow. Again, this relates to one of the tasks God gave Adam and Eve, to cultivate and keep the garden. No longer can Adam do this easily. Further, this punishment affects not only Adam but the land itself. "Cursed is the ground because of you," God says to Adam. The effects of sin are creation-wide.

The other two tasks we mentioned in Genesis 1–2, to rule over creation and to obey, were ones that Adam and Eve failed to do when they let the serpent into the garden and then fell into his temptation to eat the fruit. Their failure at these two tasks resulted in the punishments they received. But two final punishments indicate the utter seriousness of what has happened and the true effects of the sin that Adam and Eve have committed.

God finishes his punishment of Adam by telling him that he will die. From the dust of the ground he came, and to it he will return. Death—the physical separation of our soul from our body, and therefore our loss of any chance at dwelling physically in the presence of God, as we were made to do—is the ultimate punishment. God allows Adam and Eve, and their children, to experience physical separation from him. Human beings were made to dwell physically in the presence of God, and death cuts that physical presence off. And as a foretaste of this physical separation, God completes his punishment of Adam and Eve by casting them out of the garden. They cannot and will not dwell physically in the presence of God any longer.

It is vital that we see how connected the punishments for sin are to God's original design for creation. Sin does not just affect Adam and Eve's relationship to God. Of course, it *does* affect that vertical relationship; sin separates Adam and Eve and, therefore, the rest of the human race from God. But this is not sin's only effect. As we saw with Adam and Eve blaming each other and with God's punishment of Eve, and as we will see in the rest of the biblical story, sin also affects the relationships between human beings. Strife enters into Adam and Eve's relationship, and it will continue to exist between human beings as the biblical story progresses. Violence toward one another, in its various forms, exists because of sin. Adam and Eve's transgression also affects human beings in their relationship to their own bodies. Sin brings death, an unnatural state where our soul is separated from our bodies. And finally, Adam and Eve's and the entire human race's relationship to the creation is affected. The ground is cursed because of Adam. No longer does it easily bear fruit for him but, rather, bears thorns and thistles. No longer do human beings have a symbiotic relationship with the land but an antagonistic one. Sin affects *everything*.[11]

When we realize the totality of sin's effects, when we see that it affects not only a soul's relationship to God but also everything in existence, we can begin to see the scope of God's salvation that he promises in the rest of Scripture's picture of redemption. As we walk through the rest of the biblical story, it is of utmost importance that we remember what God made human beings to do—dwell with him and glorify him as his image bearers, rule, obey, multiply, and cultivate—and that each of those functions has been distorted by the fall. We also need to remember that creation itself is cursed by sin, and that all of humanity falls into Adam's inability to obey.

---

[11] On the vertical and horizontal effects of sin, and its relationship to the purposes for God's creation, see Graeme Goldsworthy, *According to Plan: An Introduction to Biblical Theology* (Downers Grove, IL: IVP Academic, 1991), 102–11.

There are, thus, two main trails that run parallel with each other and often intersect through our biblical topographical map: the fallenness of creation, and particularly the inability of Adam's descendants to obey, and the redemption that God promises to Adam and Eve in the midst of their despair in Genesis 3. Redemption is, therefore, about restoring *everything* that was lost in Genesis 1–2.[12]

Redemption

As we think about humanity's sin, we must remember that God could have left Adam and Eve in their sin and destroyed what he had made. He is God, after all! But instead, because the Lord is merciful, kind, and gracious, he gives Adam and Eve hope in the midst of administering punishments for their sin.

Hope arrives in many forms. The most obvious hope that he gives is his curse on the serpent (3:14) and his promise to Eve that her offspring will crush his head (3:15). God intends to destroy the source of evil, the serpent, and, implied in doing so, the effects of evil. God's promise to destroy the serpent is an implicit promise to redeem the world. God also gives Adam and Eve redemptive hope when he clothes them before casting them out of the garden. He gives them animal skins, which implies sacrificing an animal, a practice that is clearly associated with forgiveness of sin later in the Pentateuch (e.g., the Day of Atonement in Leviticus 16). Finally, he casts them out of the garden and allows death to loom. While these are punishments for sin, they function as signs of God's mercy as well. God exiling Adam and Eve from the garden means they no longer have access to the tree of life, which in turns mean they

---

[12] Or, as Michael Williams puts it, "The goal of redemption is nothing less than the restoration of the entire cosmos." *Far as the Curse Is Found*, 276.

cannot choose to eat its fruit and be caught in an eternal state separated from God. Death likewise is merciful, in that their bodies, now affected by and the transmitters of sinful human nature, will one day be cast off and (as we see later in the biblical story) therefore be able to be resurrected in glory to once again dwell with God physically.

Redemption Promised

Adam's Descendants (Genesis 4–11)

The most important of these signs of God's mercy is his promise that one day Eve's seed (child) will crush the serpent's head (3:15). The remainder of the book of Genesis depicts the search for this coming child, or "seed." As we read along, readers might wonder if it will be Adam and Eve's son, Seth (Genesis 5), who will be the coming child who will turn back the curse of sin. Or we wonder if the child will be the descendant of Seth, the man named Noah (Genesis 6–9).

Noah is significant in Genesis 1–11, and in Genesis 6–9 we see that God initially sets out to destroy the entire earth by a flood because of human sin. He chooses, however, to save a remnant, Noah and his family, by instructing him to build a big boat called an "ark." That ark also contains two of every kind of animal. After forty days and forty nights of flooding rain, the waters relent, and then Noah eventually finds dry land. When he steps off the boat, God makes a covenant with him, that he will never destroy the earth through a flood again (8:20–22; 9:8–17). He tells Noah to be fruitful and multiply and gives him commands to obey (9:1–7).

Once again, then, we see God telling the head of humanity to fill the earth with his descendants and to obey God's commands. Noah also is placed over the rest of creation in a way that sounds a bit like

Adam. Noah, in other words, looks like a new Adam.[13] We also see in Noah not only a picture of what was before but of what lies ahead because what happens to him—a remnant being saved from God's judgment through a wooden ark—pictures God's redemption of his people through the person and work of Jesus.

These two important threads—(1) salvation from God's judgment through (2) a "second Adam"—carry us through the rest of the Old Testament, and we find the first substantial instance of this pattern in the story of Noah. But, like the rest of the second Adams in the Old Testament, Noah actually isn't the seed of Gen 3:15. Just like the first Adam (and like the other Old Testament second Adams), Noah fails to obey God faithfully. He gets drunk, and Ham, the youngest of his three sons, mocks him. So we see that Noah's life only *pictures* the coming seed of Eve, but he clearly is not the one hoped for, the one through whom redemption will come. We will continue to see this pattern throughout the story of the Old Testament.

Genesis 10 and 11 follow the lineages of Noah's three sons. While Shem's line culminates in Genesis 11 with Abram, to whom we will return in a moment, Ham's line is filled with disaster. Not only does Ham's line produce many of the prominent enemies of the future nation of Israel, but in this section of Genesis Ham is also the father of the community of Babel. The inhabitants of Babel attempt to build a tower up to heaven, not so they can know God but so they can be like gods. Once again we see human beings attempting to take God's place, much like Adam and Eve in Genesis 3, and once again God responds by coming down and exiling them. God scatters

---

[13] See William J. Dumbrell, *Covenant and Creation: A Theology of the Old Testament Covenants*, Biblical and Theological Classics Library (Carlisle: Paternoster, 1984), 26–43.

these people to the ends of the earth and confuses their languages. While Adam and Eve were supposed to be fruitful and multiply and fill the earth with worshippers of God, the inhabitants of Babel are exiled to all parts of the earth because of their opposition to God. Given Cain's murderous heart, Lamech's violence, the world's sexual and violent fall into sin, and Babel's idolatry, Genesis 4–11 presents God's creation, and particularly his image bearers, as totally given over to the presence and power of sin. God is right and just to destroy what he has made.

Yet, these chapters in Genesis also reveal that God is patient, kind, and merciful. Instead of destroying everything, he chooses to keep a remnant. We saw this with Noah, we will see it again with Abram, and we see it clearly in the nation of Israel. The message of Genesis 4–11, then, is that the world is filled with sinful human beings who devote themselves to destruction, and our only hope is God's intervention through the promised seed of Eve. And as the end of Genesis 11 points out, that seed comes through the line of Abram.

Abraham's Family (Genesis 12–50)
It is difficult to overstate the importance of Abra(ha)m in the life of Israel or the story of the Bible. Abraham[14] is the father of the nation of Israel, by virtue of God calling him out of his homeland, Ur of the Chaldeans, and promising innumerable descendants. God uses Abraham and Sarah to produce his chosen people, Israel. In this historical respect, then, they both are vital to the story of Israel. But

---

[14] For ease of reading, I will use Abraham almost exclusively, instead of switching back and forth between Abram and Abraham. Likewise, I will use Sarah almost exclusively rather than Sarai. God changes Abram and Sarai's names in Genesis 17 when he covenants with them.

with respect to the story of the Bible, the search for the seed upon which we embarked in Gen 3:15, Abraham and Sarah are also crucial. Again, this is true from a strictly historical perspective; Abraham and Sarah are the progenitors of the nation of Israel, through whom the Messiah will come.

It is true, however, in a typological, narrative sense as well. The promises God makes to Abraham in Genesis 12, 15, and 17 all relate to the tasks God gave Adam and Eve in Genesis 1–2 and what was lost in Genesis 3.[15] Adam and Eve lost their dwelling place with God, but God promises Abraham the land of Canaan, the place where God will dwell with his family. Adam and Eve failed to rule over the garden, but God promises that kings will come from Abraham's line and rule over the promised land. Adam and Eve failed to obey, but God gives Abraham and his line a new law, circumcision. Adam and Eve failed to cultivate and keep the garden, and their sin resulted in the ground being cursed and bringing forth thorns and thistles. By contrast, Abraham's family will dwell in a land flowing with milk and honey, and his line is charged with its care. Adam and Eve's sin resulted in difficulty surrounding their ability to be fruitful and multiply, but Abraham and Sarah's descendants will be innumerable, like the stars in the sky or the sand on the seashore. Adam and Eve failed to trust God and instead listened to the serpent. As a result, they were cut off from God, counted as sinful. By contrast, Abraham believes God, and it is counted to him as righteousness (Gen 15:6). And Adam and Eve's sin resulted in the fall of all humanity and the curse on creation, but from Abraham's seed will be the one through whom God will redeem humanity and the cosmos.

---

[15] See Gordon J. Wenham, *Genesis 1–15*, WBC 1, ed. David A. Hubbard and Glenn W. Barker (Waco: Word Books, 1987), 291.

It is crucial that we see this relationship between what was lost with Adam and Eve's sin and what God will restore when he fulfills his covenant with Abraham. *All* that was lost by Adam and Eve will be restored through the seed of Abraham. Adam failed to rule and obey and therefore lost fruitfulness, cultivation, and dwelling; Abraham and his line will gain fruitfulness, cultivation, and dwelling in a land they rule and under a law they will be given through the coming seed of Eve who will crush the source of sin.

In other words, the salvation that God promises is holistic. We see this early in the promise to Eve in 3:15 and now more fully to Abraham in Genesis 12, 15, and 17. It encompasses all that was lost in the fall. Yes, Adam and Eve lost their ability to dwell with God physically in the garden. Yes, they were separated from him in their spirit through the presence of sin. Still, God will restore faithful human souls and bodies through the seed of woman. But this is not all that salvation does. God's salvation restores everything else that Adam lost as well, and we see this through the parallels between what Adam lost and what Abraham is promised.[16]

As we continue through the Old Testament story, and when we enter into the New Testament story, we should not let go of the breadth of the salvation that God promises to Abraham. It is creation-wide. God's mighty salvation extends, as the Christmas hymn goes, "far as the curse is found." It includes the restoration of the individual sinner's soul to God, yes, but it also includes the restoration of the ground from sin's curse, the redemption of human bodies from the sting of death, the remaking of God's people who

---

[16] On the cosmic scope of God's redemptive covenant with Abraham and its relation to Adam's original tasks, see Craig G. Bartholomew and Michael W. Goheen, *The Drama of Scripture: Finding Our Place in the Biblical Story* (Grand Rapids: Baker Academic, 2004), 53–57.

dwell with him in his place, and the restoration of human beings to their original tasks—fruitfulness, cultivation, obedience, and ruling.

Additionally, Abraham is a picture for us of how God will include people in this salvation project—it is by faith. When God first calls Abram to leave his home, his family, and everything he's ever known, Abram responds in faith. Later, when God makes his covenant with Abram in Genesis 15, he responds in faith. And when God in Genesis 22 calls Abraham to sacrifice Isaac, his only son by Sarah and the heir to the covenant promises, Abraham responds in faith. Those who, like Abraham, believe God's promises, and who believe that God alone is able to fulfill them, will be included in God's righteous people. His promises to Abraham are, therefore, a preview of the salvation the promised one will bring, and Abraham's response is a preview of how individuals are included in that coming salvation.

Much like Noah, though, Abraham is not only a second Adam in that he is a picture of the right response to God and of God's coming; he is also a second Adam in that he repeats Adam's failures. Like Adam, Abraham, when tempted with the forbidden, "listened to the voice of" his wife (Gen 3:17; 16:2) instead of to God.[17] Like Adam, Abraham cannot withstand temptation, and he disobeys on multiple occasions (e.g., trying to sell Sarah off as his sister to foreign kings, 12:10–20; 21:22–34). Thus, while Abraham is a picture of salvation, he is also a picture of humanity's fallen state. Like Adam and Noah, Abraham cannot obey. This will continue to be the main problem throughout Israel's history.

Adam, Noah, Abraham, and Israel cannot obey; they need the seed of Eve to destroy the source of sin and to obey for them. Also

---

[17] Gordon J. Wenham, *Genesis 16–50*, WBC 2, ed. David A. Hubbard and Glenn W. Barker (Waco: Word Books, 1994), 7.

like Adam and Eve and Noah, Abraham needs a sacrifice; Adam and Eve are clothed with animal skins, and Noah sacrifices to God when he covenants with him. Abraham takes Isaac up the mountain in Genesis 22, expecting to sacrifice his only son, but instead God provides the sacrifice for them. We thus see at least four patterns in Genesis 3–22: the holistic nature of salvation, the inability of Adam's seed to obey, the necessity of faith, and the need for sacrifice.

The line of Abraham continues first through his son Isaac and then through Jacob. While there is much to be gleaned from the narratives of Genesis 23–36, the story of one of Jacob's twelve sons, Joseph, will assist us most in continuing to draw these threads through the entire biblical story. Joseph is persecuted by his brothers and cast out of his land. He flees from sin in a Gentile nation (Egypt) and is imprisoned for it but then rises to second in command because he interprets the pharaoh's dreams. In those dreams, Joseph is able to distinguish between good and evil. Joseph is able to cultivate and keep the land and provide for his people, he is clothed in the image of the pharaoh, he is given a wife by Pharaoh, he is fruitful and multiples, and the land over which he rules as second in command is fruitful. Joseph's wisdom and his forgiveness of his brothers results in the reunification of Jacob's family, the twelve sons who will become the twelve heads of the tribes of Israel, and in the restoration of them from exile.

Joseph, like Noah and Abraham, looks like a second Adam,[18] but unlike Noah and Abraham, nowhere in this narrative do we see Joseph succumbing to temptation. Still, like Noah and Abraham, Joseph is not the seed; Genesis 38, one of the strangest chapters in the Bible, is inserted after Joseph is introduced to remind us (as does

---

[18] Ps 105:14–22 is an interesting later Israelite reflection on Joseph's life that draws out many of these same features of his rule in Egypt.

49:10–12) that the seed of woman comes not through Joseph's line but through Judah's. Further, Joseph does not crush the serpent's head, and he does not restore his father and brothers to the land that was promised to Abraham. So, we see that Joseph is not the promised seed.

In Genesis, then, what we see is a search for the seed that begins in 3:15, extends through Noah, and is most fully articulated to this point in the covenant God makes with Abraham. This seed will bring salvation and restore all that was lost through Adam and Eve's sin. We also see that faith is the required response and that sacrifice is needed. While Noah, Abraham, and Joseph look like the seed of woman who is to come, none of them fulfill that promise. We are still waiting for the Lion of the Tribe of Judah to come.

CHAPTER 3

The Story of the Bible, Part 2
Redemption, Continued

Redemption Pictured

The Exodus

After Abraham's great-grandsons find relief from tribulation through their anointed brother, another three and a half centuries pass before the next book, Exodus, begins. At this stage the twelve sons of Jacob have borne fruit and multiplied in Egypt, but a pharaoh who did not remember Joseph or his family now enslaves them. Further, because Pharaoh sees their growing numbers as a threat, he orders all male babies to be killed. God's people cry out for deliverance, and God begins to work in the life of his chosen servant, Moses, who at that time is an infant. After Moses's mother makes a basket for him out of wood and pitch and then floats him to safety (sounds like Noah!), Moses grows up in Pharaoh's court. As an adult, he is second in command to Pharaoh, like Joseph. But unlike Joseph, Moses does not flee from sin; instead, he murders an Egyptian who was mistreating one of his Hebrew kinsmen. Like Hagar and Ishmael, and like Israel after the Exodus, Moses flees into the wilderness, where he is nourished for forty years.

During this time God, who now reveals himself as YHWH ("I am that I am")—the God of Abraham, Isaac, and Jacob—calls Moses to deliver his people, Israel. Moses goes to Pharaoh and tells him to let Israel go, but Pharaoh refuses. Each time, that refusal is met with one of ten increasingly bad plagues; God demonstrates his power of the cosmos and the nations with these tribulations. Before the tenth and worst plague, the death of every firstborn son in Egypt, YHWH tells Israel to sacrifice a lamb and smear its blood over the door. If they do, the death angel will "pass over" their house. Moses also instructs Israel to prepare to flee Egypt immediately and to eat a meal that is indicative of the immediacy of their departure. These acts—the sacrifice of the lamb, preparation, and eating this particularly quick meal—are collectively known as the Passover. After YHWH sends his judgment on Pharaoh and Egypt, Pharaoh finally tells Israel to leave. As they do, though, Pharaoh changes his mind and pursues them to the shores of the Red Sea, where Israel is trapped between the Egyptian army and the water. God then miraculously parts the sea, Israel passes through, and then God brings the waters crashing down on the Egyptian army. Israel is saved.

The exodus is the dominant picture of salvation in the Old Testament.[1] God brings judgment on his enemies through the death of the firstborn son; those who faithfully trust in his word and who, therefore, cover themselves with the lamb's blood are saved from this judgment; God saves his people from their enemies through providing victory over them; and then he brings them through the

---

[1] See Graeme Goldsworthy, *According to Plan: An Introduction to Biblical Theology* (Downers Grove, IL: IVP Academic, 1991), 130–39.

water safely to the other side. (Notice that this also matches the pattern of Noah's ark.) This pattern provides the type for how salvation occurs in the rest of the Old Testament and for how the New Testament authors explain Jesus's work in the New Testament. When we think about salvation in the Old Testament, then, we should think of the holistic promises made to Abraham and the holistic picture provided by the exodus. Salvation restores all that Adam lost, and it is accomplished through sacrifice and victory over God's enemies.

After God delivers his people, he takes them through the waters of the Red Sea and starts them on their way to Mount Sinai. In both of these situations, Israel reveals what we've already seen with Adam, Noah, and Abraham: they cannot obey. At the shores of the Red Sea, Israel lacks faith and doubts that they've done the right thing in leaving Egypt. Afterward, in the wilderness, Israel grumbles and complains not once but twice, the first time about lacking water and the second time about lacking food. In all three of these instances, Israel doesn't believe that God will provide. In each instance, this doubt occurs immediately after YHWH has done something else miraculous for them, and each of these instances is indicative of the truth about Adam, Israel, and all of us: we cannot obey.

This basic point, reiterated throughout the Old Testament, is seen subsequently at Sinai. Israel arrives at the mountain, and God invites his people to come up Sinai and worship him there as his holy nation and royal priesthood. This appears to be another instance, like Joseph, of God providing something close to the salvation he promised to Abraham—Israel would worship Yahweh on the mountain in his presence. But Israel becomes afraid, and God tells them to stay where they are. Instead of Israel going up to worship him as his royal priesthood, God appoints mediators of his word and his presence. Moses goes up the mountain to receive God's Word to Israel, and then goes back down to give it. His brother, Aaron, mediates God's presence for Israel through serving as their high priest. Moses first gives them God's Word related to the tabernacle and priestly laws, so that Aaron and the Levites (appointed to be the priestly tribe) can mediate God's presence for Israel.

Even in this mediatorial relationship, though, Israel still fails to obey. Aaron, the one who is supposed to lead them into God's presence as the high priest, instead leads them to worship the golden calf while Moses is still up on the mountain receiving God's Word. Once again we find God's people departing from his word and worshipping the creature rather than the Creator. Like Adam and Eve distorted God's word and ate the fruit, and like Abraham chose to listen to the voice of his wife instead of God's promises when he slept with Hagar, here, too, Israel chooses to listen to the voice of their own sinful nature and worship the golden calf rather than listening to God's Word and worshipping YHWH alone.

God could choose here to destroy Israel, and, in fact, he says he will. This would be in concordance with his actions against humanity with the flood and against the inhabitants of Babel, among others. YHWH is rightfully wrathful toward sin, given his holy nature and, therefore, his inability to abide in the presence of sin. But YHWH is also a God of mercy and, through Moses's mediatorial prayer for Israel, relents from his intended destruction and, instead, promises to show mercy to his people. Notice that Aaron has failed to function as the mediator of God's presence via sacrifice, and so Moses, the prophetic mediator of God's Word, must also step in as the mediator of divine presence. Moses serves as prophet, but he also performs some priestly and kingly duties by interceding for Israel (Exodus 32–34) and leading them militarily.

A few threads come together here. First, once again we see (positively) that YHWH is about restoring what Adam and Eve lost through fulfilling his covenant with Abraham. This is the covenant thread. Second, we see that Israel cannot obey; God continues to call his people out of exile and slavery, but they continue to be unable to obey. This is the sin thread. Third, we see that salvation, defined holistically as fulfillment of the Abrahamic covenant, is achieved through victory over God's enemies and sacrifice, is given by the mercy of God, and is a covering for sin. This is the salvation thread. And fourth, we see that God's appointed servant and prophet mediates salvation. We need to tie this thread into the "seed of woman" thread we saw in Genesis, but we can't here in Exodus because Moses is of the tribe of Levi, not Judah. While he is a picture of the seed, he is not the seed.

The Law and the Wilderness

The final thread we have not yet mentioned is the fact that God responds to Israel's disobedience not just with mercy but also with law. One way to describe this narrative pattern is using the phrase "more sin, more law."[2] When Israel grumbles in the desert after God brings them through the Red Sea, he responds with mercy (i.e., giving them water and bread) and with law. He gives them a statute and rule. When Israel responds with fear about going up on Mount Sinai with him, YHWH gives them laws, namely the tabernacle and priestly laws. And when Israel worships the golden calf, he responds not only with mercy in not destroying them but also with law—what we typically know as the Mosaic or Sinaitic Law, a series of laws that stretches from Exodus 35 to Numbers 10.

This, however, is not to say that law is only negative. While the law's first two uses of restraining sin and teaching that we are

---

[2] On the narrative context of law-giving in the Pentateuch, see John Sailhamer, *The Meaning of the Pentateuch: Revelation, Composition, and Interpretation* (Downers Grove, IL: IVP Academic, 2009), 360–99.

sinners (see Gal 3:15–26) emphasize the sinful nature of human beings and their inability to obey, the law also has a positive function. Law, whether Sinaitic or otherwise, reflects God's created order. For the laws given at Sinai, that reflection is limited geographically, ethnically, and temporally—it is only the law for the geopolitical nation of Israel, in the promised land, until the Messiah comes. Nevertheless, it is still a reflection of how God made the world and how he intends it to operate. Or, as Michael Williams puts it, "The law tells Israel how to live as God's image bearers, what it means to be a kingdom of priests and a holy nation," in order to be "his vehicle of bringing blessing to the nations."[3] In other words, the law given at Sinai allows Israel to live within God's created order for the purpose of being a light to the nations. This is also true of the new-covenant stipulations, except that those new-covenant laws are not given within the context of Israel's inability to obey but in the context of restored Israel—the church—receiving the Spirit so that they can obey. The new-covenant laws are also not limited in their ethnic or geographical application; rather, they are for the whole people of God from every tribe, tongue, and nation, from Jerusalem to Judea and Samaria to the ends of the earth.

This tells us something about the Israelite law and the Sinaitic covenant. It is given in the context of disobedience and is for the purpose of preserving Israel as God takes them into the land. It also contains stipulations for both blessing and cursing, in that God tells Israel that if they disobey he will cast them out of the land and

---

[3] Michael D. Williams, *Far as the Curse Is Found: The Covenant Story of Redemption* (Phillipsburg, NJ: P&R, 2005), 149. We should also note here that the law is never intended to justify Israel before God but is rather their obedient response to the saving work he already accomplished in the Exodus. Ibid., 150.

disperse them as a nation. After giving these laws, Israel is prepared to depart for the promised land in Numbers 11.

As they begin their journey, God sends twelve spies into the land. Ten come back afraid, and only two (Joshua and Caleb) trust YHWH to deliver the land to them. Israel, fearful again, follows the ten and doubts YHWH's ability to fulfill his promises. Additionally, the clan of Korah rebels against Moses' leadership and, by extension, YHWH's leadership. God responds to these acts of disobedience and doubt by making Israel wander in the wilderness for forty years. At the end of this wandering, the first generation that YHWH led out of Egypt is dead, and only those twenty years old and younger are left alive to enter the promised land. And as the second generation is waiting on the plains of Moab to enter Canaan, once again God delivers his law to his people through Moses. Moses has recorded this speech for us in the book of Deuteronomy. And once again this Mosaic law ends with a warning; if Israel doesn't obey, they will be exiled.[4]

Deuteronomy ends with the death of Moses and the plan of succession for Joshua. The important point to note about this, other than the historical fact of Moses's death and Joshua's succession, is that Deuteronomy 34:9–12 tells us there has not arisen a prophet greater than Moses in all Israel since his death. Looking back to 18:15–22, this is exactly what Israel is supposed to be waiting for: a prophet greater than Moses. Deuteronomy 18 and 34 thus both anticipate a deliver greater than Moses,[5] one who delivers Israel from their

---

[4] On the cursing stipulations of the Sinaitic covenant, as seen in both Exodus and Deuteronomy, see Peter J. Gentry and Stephen J. Wellum, *Kingdom through Covenant: A Biblical-Theological Understanding of the Covenants* (Wheaton, IL: Crossway, 2012), 608–11, 665–66.

[5] On the "new Moses" theme in Scripture and second temple literature, see Dale C. Allison, *The New Moses: A Matthean Typology* (Eugene, OR: Wipf and Stock, 2013).

enemies and leads them into God's dwelling place. Deuteronomy, and thus the Pentateuch, ends with Israel outside the land, waiting for the prophet greater than Moses to bring them into God's place where they will dwell with him forever.

The Conquest

There is hope that Joshua will be this prophet greater than Moses; Joshua 1 describes him in many ways like Moses, and, unlike Moses, he does lead Israel into Canaan.[6] Their entry into the land looks like a new exodus: they are circumcised and celebrate Passover before entering, Joshua encounters the commander of the LORD's army in much the same way that Moses encountered YHWH in the burning bush, and the actual crossing of the Jordan sounds the same as Israel's crossing of the Red Sea. When they get to the other side, they begin to follow God's instructions to take the land from the Canaanites by attacking Jericho. This battle, too, has theological and typological overtones: marching around the city for six days then seven times on the seventh day, blowing trumpets, and the walls crashing down all bring to mind the creation and Sinai narratives. Note the following connections between Exodus and Judges:

1. The six days followed by a heightened seventh day is obviously reminiscent of creation, while the trumpets blasting is reminiscent of the theophany ("God-appearing") at Mount Sinai.
2. Further, Joshua, a new Moses, leads them to destroy God's enemies, which reminds us of God's promise to Eve to destroy the serpent.

---

[6] Stephen G. Dempster, *Dominion and Dynasty: A Theology of the Hebrew Bible*, NSBT 15, ed. D. A. Carson (Downers Grove, IL: IVP, 2003), 128.

Israel's entry into the land in Judges thus thematically reminds us of creation, the Exodus, and Mount Sinai—it is a new creation for Israel, a new beginning.

However, as with Adam, Noah, Abraham, and Israel at Sinai, almost immediately after God's people are in God's land and expected to obey his law, they disobey. We see this in the story of Achan (Josh 7:16–26). Instead of following God's command to refrain from keeping the spoils of battle, Achan takes some bounty and hides it away. This act of disobedience results in Israel's defeat at Ai. They have disobeyed God and trusted their own judgment, and therefore the LORD's hand is not with them in battle. Much like Adam and Eve eating the forbidden fruit results in their punishment by YHWH, so Achan touches and takes something that is forbidden and God's people are punished as a result. While they are not exiled from the land, this punishment foreshadows ominous things to come for Israel.[7]

The rest of the book of Joshua is taken up with Israel's continued march through the land. In the book, we see that sometimes they are obedient and victorious, but other times they are not. What is evident is that Israel continues to exist, in spite of their sin, only because of God's mercy and grace toward them. Joshua reveals that Israel behaves like the nations: they refuse to obey their God. But Joshua includes that, despite their sin, God has chosen to redeem them for the sake of the nations (Joshua 6).

At the end of the book of Joshua, he gives a final speech before his death, much like Moses did at the end of Deuteronomy. In it Joshua exhorts Israel to obey God's law, and Israel affirms they will do just that (24:16–21). But Joshua wonders aloud whether they will keep their word (v. 19). Israel's history of disobedience, and

---

[7] William J. Dumbrell, *The Faith of Israel: A Theological Survey of the Old Testament*, 2nd ed. (Grand Rapids: Baker Academic, 2002), 73.

Joshua's doubt in the face of their commitment, should make us think that Israel's commitment will not last.

This failure of commitment and fidelity to YHWH is exactly what occurs in the book of Judges. Israel continually falls into sin, worships idols, and then receives God's judgment at the hands of a foreign oppressor. When they experience oppression, they cry out to YHWH, who sends a deliverer, or judge. After the judge casts off the oppressor through (often miraculous) military victory, the people and the land rest, usually for forty years. This process is called "the cycle" among scholars. We see it clearly in Judges 2:11–23. None of the judges are particularly exemplary (except maybe Deborah), and most of them are morally suspect if not bankrupt (especially Sampson!).

By the end of the book of Judges, things have proceeded in a downward spiral into communal sin. Israel is in a civil war because men from the tribe of Benjamin rape a Levite's concubine (Judges 19). It is fascinating that this story shares so many similarities to the story of the visitors to Lot's house in Sodom from Genesis 19. After the men of Benjamin rape the Levite's concubine, the priest finds her dead and laying at the threshold of the house in which he was staying. With cold heartlessness, he chops her up into twelve pieces and sends them to the twelve tribes, who are then incensed at Benjamin. Led by the tribe of Judah, all Israel comes against the tribe of Benjamin, and God tells them to destroy that tribe. The instruction is reminiscent of God's instruction to totally destroy the Canaanite tribes when they enter the land in Joshua. Instead of doing so, Israel chooses once again to disobey. They deprive Benjamin of being able to marry from within their own tribe as a kind of punishment, but then they also supply the men of Benjamin with foreign wives. This is double disobedience: first, by not wiping out Benjamin as God instructed, and second, by allowing to intermarry, something the Mosaic law expressly forbids. This is not because God affirms ethnic purity or racism but because he knew that, in marrying Canaanites, Israel would fall into worshipping their spouses' idols. This is exactly what happens throughout the period of the judges recorded in the book of Judges. Israel chooses to disobey God's law and worship idols instead of YHWH. They reject God's word and God's love, just like Adam and Eve did in Genesis 3.

The picture at the end of Judges is, thus, incredibly dire. The refrain appears throughout Judges 17–21 that "There was no king in Israel" and "the people did what was right in their own eyes." Israel has rejected God as their King, and they, therefore, reject his Word that should govern them. This refrain points to the necessary solution—Israel recognizing YHWH as their King. And the next (and last) books of Israel's primary history, Samuel and Kings, tell us about the rise and fall of kings in Israel.[8]

The Davidic Kingdom

Samuel begins like Judges ended: there is no king in Israel, nor is there any word from God, and the high priest's sons are acting like pagans. Like in Judges, only God's merciful, miraculous intervention can save Israel, and he provides Samuel, the last of Israel's judges. Samuel leads Israel to military victory over their constant enemy, Palestine, but the people still clamber for a king, one "like the nations" and not YHWH. This is a negative request; Israel continues to desire the creation over the Creator. Instead of recognizing YHWH's merciful and gracious kingship over them, they want a king who can militarily make them lord over the nations. And so God gives them what they request in Saul of the tribe of Benjamin

---

[8] On Judges, see David Beldman, *Deserting the Crown: The Book of Judges*, Transformative Word, ed. Craig G. Bartholomew (Bellingham, WA: Lexham, 2016).

(not the best tribe given the end of Judges!). Saul, in short, looks the part but does not play it. He is a bad shepherd (the first story we hear of him is how he lost his father's donkeys), he is a bad king (he makes a rash vow before battle), he is a bad priest (he makes the sacrifice instead of Samuel), and he is a bad prophet (he doesn't listen to God's word regarding the complete destruction of the Agagites). He is the opposite of Moses and, therefore, decidedly not what Israel should be waiting for.[9]

After Saul directly ignores God's word regarding the Agagites, the Spirit of YHWH moves from Saul to David from the tribe of Judah. David is first pictured as a good shepherd. We then see him achieve YHWH-governed, miraculous victory as God's representative for Israel over Goliath, the representative of God's enemies, the Philistines, through seemingly foolish means. David is a good shepherd and now serves as a good king. Typologically David foreshadows Israel's future redeemer: the One who will crush God's enemies and deliver them. The narrative reveals David function as a good quasipriest (2 Samuel 5) and a quasiprophet, in that he speaks God's word to his people.

David even heightens our expectations for the coming Messiah. The text says that David conquers all the enemies surrounding Israel (2 Samuel 10) and receives a royal covenant from YHWH in 2 Samuel 7. This covenant expands on the ones made to Abraham and to Israel, promising that a son of David will sit on the throne forever and that this same son of David will build YHWH's house. David, thus, reminds us of the promised seed of Eve and of the fulfillment of Abraham's covenant but now also adds to our expectation that his son will reign forever and build the temple, God's dwelling place

---

[9] For a good introduction to 1–2 Samuel, see: Heath A. Thomas and J. D. Greear, *Exalting Jesus in 1–2 Samuel*, CCEC (Nashville, TN: Holman Reference, 2016).

with his people. But however much David looks to be the fulfillment of God's promises, we must recognize that he is not the promised "seed" of Gen 3:15. Like Adam, Noah, Abraham, and Israel, David, too, falls into sin by claiming something that is not his, and that is forbidden in God's law. He takes another man's wife, Bathsheba, and then kills her husband, Uriah the Hittite. David's fall into sin casts him and his house into turmoil. Second Samuel 11–24 details the descent of the house of David: his children turn on him; three of them die; and one of those, Absalom, casts Israel into civil war.[10] David's story at the end is a tragedy rather than a triumph.

At the conclusion of this turmoil, Solomon emerges as David's heir to the throne in 1 Kings 1–2. After his coronation, Solomon constructs the temple and places the ark in it. The temple is described in 1 Kings 7 as a new garden of Eden, and so with its completion, Solomon, along with all Israel, is pictured as a new Adam, dwelling with God in his garden-temple, with rest from their enemies all around.

The Divided Kingdom and the Exile

Despite some bright spots, the story of Solomon and Israel continues as a story of failure in fidelity to God. Solomon, like his father and like Abraham, Noah, and Adam, fails. He cannot obey. He touches what is forbidden and worships the creature rather than the Creator by taking on foreign (idol-worshipping) wives. God's punishment for Solomon's sin is to divide the kingdom of Israel in half. While we may hope that Solomon would be the new Adam and the promised Son of David, the text reveals that he rips God's kingdom apart through his idolatry.

---

[10] On 1–2 Samuel, see Peter J. Leithart, *A Son to Me: An Exposition of 1–2 Samuel* (Moscow, ID: Canon, 2003).

The rest of the books of Kings (1 Kings 12–2 Kings 25) is the story of Israel's decline and fall into exile. The endless succession of kings in both the northern and southern kingdoms, most of whom are idolaters and rebellious against YHWH, is dizzying. The only hope Israel has is found once again in the prophetic word of YHWH, delivered in 1 Kings 17–2 Kings 9 by God's prophets, Elijah and Elisha. In fact, when one looks at the structure of 1–2 Kings, the ministry of Elijah and Elisha sits right in the middle of those books, highlighting the importance of God's Word and the prophetic call to repent. Those who repent and believe God's Word are saved from destruction, including kings like Hezekiah and Josiah. But most of Israel in the north and Judah in the south is not like this repentant remnant. Most of the Israelites, including their kings, are idol worshippers and rebellious against God.

And so YHWH casts Israel out of the land for the rebellion, just like he cast Adam and Eve out of the garden and just as he prophesied in the books of Deuteronomy and Joshua. First Assyria comes in and destroys the northern kingdom in 722 BC, and then Nebuchadnezzar and Babylon come in and destroy the southern kingdom, and with it Jerusalem and the temple, in 586 BC. God's people failed to obey God's law, failed to rule in the fear of the Lord, failed to cultivate and keep the land, and failed to multiply worshippers of YHWH through turning to idols and turning their children toward idols. They are, thus, once again cast out of God's place.

There is a kind of *inclusio*, or a set of bookends, around Israel's story. On one end you have Adam and Eve dwelling in the garden and then cast out of it because of disobedience, but accompanied by a prophecy of their salvation (Genesis 1–3). On the other end you have Israel dwelling in the land with the garden-temple at its center and then exiled because of disobedience (1–2 Kings).[11] What hope would Israel have to be delivered from their sin?

Redemption Prophesied

Hope comes in the message of the prophets. Like Adam and Eve, though, exile is not the final word. God's prophets speak a hopeful word for the future. There is much we could say here about the prophetic books in the Old Testament, but suffice it to say that they are both covenant lawyers, showing Israel how they are guilty of breaking God's covenant law, and at the same time prophetic ministers, giving Israel hope that YHWH will save his people and return them from exile in the future. It is on this latter ministry that we will focus here. And while a book-by-book survey of each prophet would be helpful, at this stage it will be best to summarize what the prophets state is Israel's hope.

G. K. Beale provides a helpful summary of the hope that the Old Testament prophets declare regarding the "last days." This phrase refers to the period in which YHWH will return and redeem Israel from exile by conquering their enemies and restoring the promised land. According to Beale, YHWH will do the following ten things for Israel "in the last days":

1. A final, unsurpassed and incomparable period of tribulation for God's people by an end-time opponent who deceives and

---

[11] On Kings, see Peter J. Leithart, *1 & 2 Kings*, BTCB, ed. R. R. Reno (Grand Rapids: Brazos, 2006). On Chronicles, which covers much of the same material but with distinct theological points to make, see Scott Hahn, *The Kingdom of God as Liturgical Empire: A Theological Commentary on 1–2 Chronicles* (Grand Rapids: Baker Academic, 2012).

persecutes, in the face of which they will need wisdom not to compromise; afterward they are
2. Delivered,
3. Resurrected, and their kingdom established;
4. At this future time, God will rule on earth
5. Through a coming Davidic king who defeats all opposition and reign in peace in a new creation over both
6. The nations and
7. Restored Israel,
8. With whom God will make a new covenant, and
9. Upon whom God will bestow the Spirit, and
10. Among whom the Temple will be rebuilt.[12]

These ten promises are a succinct summary of the promises of the Old Testament prophets. While each of them uses different imagery to describe these promises, Beale's list accurately captures what they promise as a whole.

The important point for us to see here is how they are connected back to the story we have just rehearsed: the story from Genesis 1 to 1 Kings 25, which is a story from creation to exile. Notice how Beale's list corresponds to what Israel and the world have been expecting: YHWH will rule in his renewed people's midst through his Messiah, the Son of David and Suffering Servant. Those who experience God's renewal and restoration are those who repent and believe in YHWH's Messiah. This is true whether you are a descendant of Abraham or whether you are one of the "nations." But whether Israel or the nations, those who do not repent and believe are destined for destruction.

---

[12] G. K. Beale, *A New Testament Biblical Theology: The Unfolding of the Old Testament in the New* (Grand Rapids: Baker Academic, 2011), 187.

Sin will be forgiven through sacrifice, death will be defeated through resurrection, and God will gain victory over all his enemies. His people, those who turn to him in faith, will once again be able to dwell with him in his place, being fruitful and multiplying among the nations, ruling with him, caring for his creation, and obeying his Word because they have his Spirit dwelling in them. All of this can be succinctly summarized as "return from exile." This is what Israel, and by extension the world, is waiting for between Malachi and Matthew.

CHAPTER 4

The Story of the Bible, Part 3
The New Testament

When the pages of the New Testament open on Matthew 1, Israel is still in exile. This statement seems odd, especially when we know that God's people did return to their land, as Jeremiah prophesied and Ezra–Nehemiah makes clear. But what kind of return was it? Well, it was far from the glorious return Israel had envisioned.

While King Cyrus of Persia allowed Israel to return to their land and rebuild the temple seventy years after Nebuchadnezzar destroyed Jerusalem, the books of Ezra–Nehemiah, Chronicles, Haggai, Zechariah, and Malachi all make clear that Israel still remains in exile. After they returned to the land after the exile, Ezra prays,

> "Even in our slavery [under Persian overlords], God has
> given us a little relief and a light to our eyes. Though we
> are slaves, our God has not abandoned us in our slavery.
> He has extended grace to us in the presence of the Persian
> kings, giving us relief, so that we can rebuild the house of

our God and repair its ruins, to give us a wall in Judah and
Jerusalem." (Ezra 9:8–9 CSB)

This is not the glorious return God's people anticipated. They
still sit under foreign rule, as slaves, and they still battle the problem
of sin. As Ezra says, his people remain defiled before God with the
guilt of sin (9:10–15). In this way, God's people are in exile apart
from the promised return anticipated in Jeremiah 31–33.

Moreover, a number of other features points to Israel's continued exile, despite returning to the land. The second temple does
not have the glory of the former Solomonic temple. Israel continues
to disobey YHWH. Israel continues to be oppressed by a series of
foreign kingdoms from the time of Ezra, culminating with Roman
rule beginning in 67 BC. Even worse than Rome being sovereign,
though, is the fact that Israel's ruling class, and especially Herod and
the Sadduccees, aligned itself with the emperor. Israel does not pos-
sess the land under its own power, the rebuilt temple does not match
the glory of the first, the ruler of God's people is not a Son of David,
and God's people are oppressed by Rome. In these ways, Israel still
sits in exile, despite dwelling in the promised land.[1]

Redemption Accomplished

It is in this desperate situation that we find YHWH once again
acting to save his people but this time decisively and finally. Like
in the period of the Judges, Israel is under foreign oppression, Israel does not have a king or a temple, and Israel is waiting on a

---

[1] For further discussion on Israel in exile in the time of the New Testament, see
N. T. Wright, *The New Testament and the People of God*, Christian Origins 1 (Minneapolis: Fortress, 1992).

word from the LORD. And as he did in the books of 1–2 Samuel and 1–2 Kings, YHWH now will deliver Israel from their enemies, provide Israel with a king and temple, and give his people his word through his coming prophet. Most importantly, this time, YHWH will come down himself and accomplish all of this for his people, and he will do it by becoming one of them. Theologians have a name for that time when God becomes one of his people in order to redeem the world: the *incarnation*, which comes from the Latin and literally means "in-the-flesh." And God becomes incarnate in his one and only Son, Jesus the Messiah. The incarnation of God in the person of Jesus Christ is the fulfillment of Israel's story and, thereby, the story of the whole world.[2]

When Jesus comes, he comes as God in the flesh to restore Israel and to restore the world. We see this particularly in Jesus's baptism. Jesus crosses the Jordan, like Israel did under Joshua's leadership and echoing the exodus crossing of the Red Sea; and as John baptizes him, the Spirit descends on him (see Isa 64:1),[3] and the Father says, "This is my beloved Son, with whom I am well pleased" (Matt 3:17). The first half of that statement is an allusion to Ps 2:7, while the latter half is an allusion to Isa 53:10.[4] Jesus is, thus, pictured also as the new Moses, the prophet of God leading his people through the waters of the Jordan. Jesus is pictured as the new David, the messianic King who will rule the nations. Jesus is pictured as the Suffering Servant, the priest who will make the sacrifice for Israel's sins. Jesus is the true Israel. Although he is tempted

---

[2] See Craig G. Bartholomew and Michael W. Goheen, *The Drama of Scripture: Finding Our Place in the Biblical Story* (Grand Rapids: Baker Academic, 2004), 129–70.

[3] See Rikki Watts, *Isaiah's New Exodus in Mark*, Biblical Studies Library (Grand Rapids: Baker Academic, 2000), 102–18.

[4] Ibid., 109.

in the wilderness, unlike Israel, Jesus obeys the Father. Jesus is the new Moses, the new David, the High Priest, and the new Israel. All that the prophets promised finds fulfillment in him. All that Adam, Abraham, Israel, and the world have been waiting for comes to fruition in his life, ministry, death, resurrection, ascension, and gift of the Spirit at Pentecost.[5]

Consider what Jesus's coming to the world means in the biblical story. His work consummates and fulfills all of God's promises in the past: to Adam and Eve, to Abraham, and to Israel. In fact, we can think about Jesus's life as fulfilling Israel's hope as articulated in the Old Testament.[6] Most importantly, Jesus atones for sin and provides victory over God's enemies—the serpent, sin, and death. In his atoning death, Jesus takes the punishment for humanity's sin. He is the sacrificial Lamb not just for Israel but for all of God's people, those who believe from every tribe, tongue, and nation. He is the Suffering Servant, promised by Isaiah, the one through whom Israel's sins are forgiven. Jesus is the High Priest for those who believe, offering himself as a perfect sacrifice on the cross for their atonement so that they, too, have access to God's throne room. In his resurrection he puts death to death, the final blow in its devastating defeat at the hands of Christ. In his death and resurrection, Jesus pays the penalty for sin and defeats sin, death, and the serpent. He is the promised seed of woman, the One who would restore what Adam and Eve lost in the fall.

---

[5] On these themes see G. K. Beale, *A New Testament Biblical Theology: The Unfolding of the Old Testament in the New* (Grand Rapids: Baker Academic, 2011), 129–86; and Matthew Y. Emerson, *Christ and the New Creation: A Canonical Approach to the Theology of the New Testament* (Eugene, OR: Wipf and Stock, 2013), 44–60.

[6] In chap. 3 of this book, see the list by Beale.

This is vital to understand—Jesus's atoning death and victorious resurrection are part of a bigger picture, one in which Jesus not only provides forgiveness for sin but also restores all that Adam and Eve lost. This includes not only an individual relationship with God but also the tasks, or purposes, God gave to Adam and Eve in the garden: to dwell with him in the land and rule it, to be fruitful and multiply, to cultivate and keep his place, and to obey his word. Jesus does not merely take our punishment; he restores those who believe to what God made them to be in the garden. In the following sections, we will see how Christ's work in his life, death, resurrection, and ascension redeem Adam's race from the curse of sin and also restores humanity to the four tasks and purposes God gave them in the garden: ruling and dwelling, obeying, cultivating, and multiplying.

Ruling and Dwelling

Jesus, as Israel's Messiah, restores the rule of the Davidic Son, as the Father establishes his throne at his right hand forever. Jesus demonstrates his authority throughout his earthly ministry, casting out demons, performing miracles, calling his disciples, teaching, and interpreting the law. He is a prophet-king, performing miracles, delivering God's Word, and calling God's people out from the nations through that same Word. He is also Israel's King, the One to whom the law of Moses and the prophets like Elijah point. We see this especially on the Mount of Transfiguration, where Moses and Elijah both sit at the feet of Jesus in all of his divine glory. We also see Jesus's authority over Israel in his calling of the twelve disciples; the number twelve is clearly intended to evoke the twelve tribes. Jesus is remaking Israel around himself as the Davidic Son (e.g., Luke 1:32; 3:31; 18:38–39).

Ultimately, Jesus's authority as the Davidic King is demonstrated in his ascension. After his resurrection, Jesus spends forty days teaching his disciples how to read their Scriptures in light of him. At the end of this period, he ascends into heaven, where he is now seated at the right of the Father, ruling and reigning over all things until his return. He is King not over Israel only but also over the whole world, over his own people and all the peoples, over those who believe and those who actively oppose him. The world is now his footstool; all things are under his feet (Eph 1:20–21). Jesus is the better David, who rules over Israel and the world and who puts under his feet not just a few nations surrounding Israel but the entire world.

Of course, Adam, Abraham, David, and Solomon's rule is instituted so that God's image bearers can dwell with him. As Jesus reigns over all things, then, he fulfills this goal for right rule, in that he is the dwelling place of God with humanity and, through his Spirit, resides always with his people. First, Jesus is the restored Temple. In his incarnation, God himself "tabernacles" among us (John 1:14), and Jesus makes explicit in the temple narrative of John 2 that he, in his resurrection, is the fulfillment of God's promise to return Israel from exile by rebuilding the temple. YHWH once again dwells in the midst of his people in the person of Jesus Christ. And in his ascension, Jesus now sits at the right of the Father, our mediator in the throne room of God, and he also sends his Spirit to dwell in those who repent and believe at Pentecost and upon profession of faith for every believer since. So, Jesus is the embodiment of the temple, dwells now as our mediator in the heavenly temple, and sends his Spirit on us so that we, too, are in and part of this new temple.[7]

---

[7] See G. K. Beale, *The Temple and the Church's Mission: A Biblical Theology of the Dwelling Place of God*, NSBT (Grand Rapids: IVP, 2004), 162–200, 245–68.

Obeying

Like Adam, Abraham, and Israel, Jesus, in his humanity, is expected to obey God's law. Unlike Adam, Abraham, Israel, and all of us, though, Jesus does in fact obey God's law. While he is tempted as we are in every respect, he does not sin. As the messianic Son of David, he is anointed and guided by the Spirit of God. As the God-Man, in his humanity he is tempted, but in his divinity he cannot sin. Jesus is, therefore, what the world has needed since the beginning: a second Adam, the head of a new humanity who does not cast them into sin through his disobedience like the first Adam but instead obeys on their behalf. He redeems humanity from the power of sin through reversing the course of the fall in his human obedience. And he obeys as God's chosen servant, the new Israel, being tempted in the wilderness (Matt 4:1–11) but refusing to sin; this reverses the course of Israel's life, whose main issue in the Old Testament was that they could not obey. Jesus here takes Israel's place and in doing so takes humanity's place—and obeys for all those who repent and believe.

Cultivating

At first glance, perhaps the most difficult task to think about Jesus fulfilling is Adam and Eve's role as cultivators and keepers of the garden. And yet, if we read the Gospels closely, we find him doing just that. Jesus, especially in his miracles and resurrection, is not only renewing his people and redeeming them from sin but also restoring the world. He demonstrates his authority over nature, particularly in walking on water and calming the storm (Mark 4:35–41).

Perhaps more importantly for the current point, he not only demonstrates his authority over but also renews the fallen creation through his miracles. So, when he heals the blind man or raises the little girl and Lazarus from the dead or causes the lame to walk or the deaf to hear, these are not just proofs of his divinity and messianic status. They are the in-breaking of the restoration of creation, to be consummated at Christ's return, into the fallen creation. Christ is healing the material world, the cosmos, through his miracles. Of course the ultimate restoration of the world comes in Jesus' resurrection. The new Adam is raised to new life, and through his headship over all creation is the firstfruits of creation's redemption as well. Right now creation groans for that coming restoration (Rom 8:22–23), but its deposit has been made in the resurrection of Jesus from the dead. Jesus cultivates and keeps the land through his miracles and his resurrection. (It is no accident that Mary mistakes him for a gardener [John 20:15] after he rises!)

Multiplying

Jesus is also fruitful and multiplies his people, not under the curse but as redeemed women and men. He does so in a few ways. First, he sends his Spirit on his people, making them new Adams and Eves as well. In John 20:22, Jesus breathes his spirit into his disciples, a clear allusion to Gen 2:7 when God breathes life into Adam and Eve. At Pentecost, he remakes his people and reverses the punishment of Babel, creating a new people of God through the power of his Spirit.

The second way that Jesus is fruitful and multiples is through calling disciples. Specifically, Jesus, in calling twelve disciples, is remaking Israel and then sending them into the world to make more disciples (Luke 10:1–12). This was the purpose of Adam and Abraham and Israel, to make more image bearers of YHWH throughout the earth. Whereas they failed or did not complete that task, Jesus here remakes Adam and Abraham's seed, Israel, through his own life and also through the calling of disciples. He then sends them out to do what Israel did not finish: to be a light to the nations and to bring the nations in to worship YHWH with them.

This is the third way that Jesus is fruitful and multiplies, by sending his Spirit-renewed, called-out disciples into the world on mission. Jesus calls his new Israel to share the good news of his life, death, and resurrection with Jew and Gentile. He sends them out to "feed his sheep" (John 21:15–19), to "go and make disciples of all nations" (Matt 28:19), and to be his "witnesses in Jerusalem and in all Judea and Samaria, and to the end of the earth" (Acts 1:8). As the church is birthed and sent in Acts, God begins to fulfill his intent for creation: to fill it with image-bearing worshippers of him, who will rule in and cultivate the place he made for them, and to dwell with them there.

The Already/Not Yet Structure

While "all the promises of God find their 'yes' in Christ Jesus" (2 Cor 1:20), and while Jesus has accomplished all that needs to be accomplished in his life, death, resurrection, ascension, and gift of the Spirit, there is still a sense in which we are waiting for salvation's completion. Theologians call this twofold sense of Christ's work the "already/not yet" structure of the New Testament.

Jesus has already finished the work of salvation, but he has not yet consummated it. When he returns in glory, he will complete what he began in Matthew 1. The easiest way to see this is by looking at how Jesus multiplies his people through his Spirit. In one sense, the conversion of Gentiles in the Gospels and Acts fulfills God's promises to save the nations on the last day. But in another sense, that evangelistic mission to the nations is ongoing. There are nations that have not yet heard the gospel, and so God's mission continues. Or we could think about Jesus's death and resurrection; in that act, he has fully defeated Satan and all God's adversaries, placing them under his feet. Salvation is already accomplished. But in another sense, we are still waiting for Satan to not just suffer defeat (which he has) but to be destroyed completely. This will not occur until Christ's return.

A common illustration for this already/not yet structure is the difference between D-Day and V-Day in World War II. When the Allied Forces stormed the beaches of Normandy, the war on the Western front was effectively over. The victory was in hand, and the Germans and their allies were not going to be able to come back. But, as they retreated, they still attacked the Allies in skirmishes. There were still battles to be fought even though the war had been won because the enemy had been defeated but not destroyed. That is why V-Day is so important; on that day, when the treaty was signed, the Nazis not only suffered defeat but also were effectively destroyed, not in a physical sense but in the sense that they were no longer an existent, hostile military force.

Jesus has stormed the forces of Satan in his life, death, resurrection, ascension, and gift of the Spirit; he has crushed the serpent's head; he has put all God's enemies under his feet. And yet, we are still waiting for the final consummation of that already-won victory: the total destruction of his enemies and the renewal of the world and his people at his return. It is in this period, between the times, that the church waits in hope for Christ's second coming.[8]

Redemption Applied

While Christ's church waits between the times, the mission to the nations is her goal. She is to go into all nations and make disciples, as

---

[8] For a brief overview of Jesus's inauguration of the new creation, and how we still wait for its completion, see Graeme Goldsworthy, *According to Plan: An Introduction to Biblical Theology* (Downers Grove, IL: IVP Academic, 1991), 201–9.

Jesus told his disciples in Matt 28:18. Note that "mission" includes evangelism—sharing the good news of Jesus with those who have not yet repented of their sins and believed—but it is more than that. Mission is about making disciples. Discipleship does not end with conversion but, rather, begins there. Thus, the book of Acts and the letters of the New Testament, both Pauline and General, are about the church being fruitful and multiplying through making disciples.

Acts and the New Testament Letters describe the church and its task in a number of ways. First, the church is the embodied recipient and proclaimer of Christ's work through the power of his Spirit.[9] The church is the body of Christ, participating in his rule with him but, like Adam, as vice regents, under his authority while also exercising his authority. Just as Christ sits in the heavenly places, ruling over every power, principle, and authority (Eph 1:20–21), so too the church now is seated in the heavenly places, ruling with Christ (2:6). The church, united to Christ and indwelt by his Spirit, is now the temple of God through that Spirit-union with Christ, who through his incarnation is the place where God dwells with his people (John 1:14; 2:21). In other words, as we are united to Christ, who is the Temple of God, we too become the temple, the place where God's Spirit dwells with his people.

We could go on, but the point is that Christ's accomplishments are now applied to us, first in the sense that those who repent and believe in Christ's work alone to save are justified before God but also in the sense that Christ applies his entire work—not only the work of atonement—to the life of the church. As we are united to him by faith in his Spirit, that same Spirit applies Christ's work to us. So we now, too, participate with Christ in his works of obedience,

---

[9] On the theological themes of Acts, see my *Christ and the New Creation*, 60–63; and Goldsworthy, *According to Plan*, 210–16.

cultivation, being fruitful and multiplying, and ruling. We are participating in Adam and Eve's task of multiplying because the church is the body of the new Adam. Jesus in his person and work restores humanity, and everyone who is united to him by faith participates in that renewal of God's image bearers. Christ accomplished what Adam and Israel could not, and now we, as the new people of God—Jew and Gentile united as the renewed Israel (Rom 9:6–7)—participate in those tasks that he gave to Adam and Israel and which have been fulfilled in Christ.

Second, the church is to participate in these tasks predominantly through (1) becoming more like Christ by the power of his Spirit to the glory of the Father and (2) proclaiming Christ to the nations by the power of his Spirit to the glory of the Father. The Letters encourage Christians to do this in two ways: by looking back to Christ's death and resurrection and by looking forward to Christ's return. Because Christ died and rose again, believers are freed from the power of sin and can, therefore, pursue righteousness, grow in the knowledge of God, and pass on sound teaching by the power of the Holy Spirit. And because Christ died and rose again, believers are now Christ's ambassadors to the world, proclaiming that good news to all people and calling on them to repent and believe by the power of the Holy Spirit. Looking forward, because Christ will return to judge the living and the dead, Christians can now live holy and upright lives and combat false teaching by the power of his Spirit. And they are to proclaim Christ's return to a lost and dying world by the power of his Spirit because all people will, on that day, face his judgment. This is what it means to live between the times of Christ's first and second coming. We pursue Christlikeness in our character and in our doctrine so that we can proclaim Christ rightly to a lost and dying world. And we do so because Christ died and rose again and because he will one day return in glory.

The third way that the New Testament Letters speak of this already/not yet period is more somber. James and Peter both use the term "exile," and many of the letters speak of believers experiencing trial, tribulation, and trouble in this present age. While Christ has accomplished all that God has promised, we are still waiting for the consummation of that work. Until then, in a sense we are still in exile, waiting for the heavenly city that is to come (Heb 13:14). This is how Revelation describes this period, as one in which believers are to remain faithful to God in Christ by his Spirit in the midst of tribulation because he is ruling now and will return soon. Suffering, trials, persecution, and death may come, but God is faithful to his people. One day he will return, and his people will no longer be waiting for the city; the city will come down to them (Rev 21:1). While we wait, while we make disciples and grow as disciples, while we proclaim the gospel to the world, while we suffer and die, we do so with hope. We hope, not in futility but with certainty, that one day Christ will return, that we will dwell with him, and that he will consummate what he accomplished in his first coming.[10]

Redemption Consummated

It is on the day when Christ returns that his work of redemption, the accomplishment of YHWH's plan of salvation, will be consummated. In Rev 20:7–22:16, we see God's plan of salvation culminating with the return of Christ, the final judgment, and the new heavens and new earth. At Christ's second coming, the divine Judge will judge all humanity. Those who repented and believed in Christ's

---

[10] On the Epistles and their relation to the story line, see Vaughn Roberts, *God's Big Picture: Tracing the Storyline of the Bible* (Downers Grove, IL: IVP, 2003), 129–45.

work will dwell with God for eternity in the new heavens and new earth, and those who did not will be cast into the lake of fire (20:7–15; 21:8). And when Jesus casts the serpent in the lake of fire in Rev 20:10, it is the completion of the victory he won over the serpent in his life, death, resurrection, and ascension.

Unlike the first Adam, the second Adam, Jesus, rules well and defeats the serpent instead of letting him enter God's place. This proper rule by Jesus leads to the purpose of rule to begin with: to be able to dwell with God in his place and without the power or presence of sin. And this is what occurs next, after Jesus rules well in his final judgment: he brings his people into God's place, the new heavens and new earth. At last, exile is no more.

This new heavens and new earth is not some spiritual, ghostly otherworld where we all sit around, bodiless (although how can you sit without a body?) on our individual cloud with togas and lyres singing "Lord, I lift your name on high" for all eternity. No, John's Apocalypse describes the new heavens and new earth as a renewal, a restoration, of the creation that already exists. This is the culmination of the biblical story. What was lost in Genesis 3 will be restored in Revelation 21–22. And remember, the fall affected not only humanity; it affected all of creation. Therefore, when Jesus comes back to finish what he started, he restores not just human beings but the creation in which they are meant to dwell. "Heaven," as we like to call it, is real. It is earth-y because it is this earth, this cosmos, renewed from the effects of sin and freed from its presence because of Jesus's right rule. The new heavens and new earth is a real place—a physical, material place—because it is simply this world, this universe, renewed and restored. And it is God's dwelling place, the place where his people will live with him for all eternity (Rev 21:4).

The new heavens and new earth is also a good place, a place that is sustaining for and cultivated by those who dwell with God in it. Revelation 21–22 describes the "new heavens and new earth" as a city (new Jerusalem) with a beautiful, extensive garden in the midst of it, where God dwells, like he did in Israel's temple. God's image bearers, who are now the inhabitants of the heavenly city, cultivate and keep this holy city, whether by bringing gifts into the sanctuary (21:24—27) or through consuming the good fruit of the land for the healing of the nations (22:2). Much like the Old Testament priests were required to do with the temple, the new residents also do not bring anything unclean into the holy city, thus ruling and cultivating well (21:27; 22:3–5). Further, this refusal and inability to bring any-thing unclean into the city-temple, and to walk in the light and not in the darkness, is the culmination of Christ's obedience and his gift of the Spirit. Because he has obeyed for those of us who have repented and believed, we are allowed into this new creation, and because he has given us his Spirit and banished the serpent and sin, we can obey the LORD forever in the new heavens and new earth.

Finally, now that Jesus has ruled, obeyed, and cultivated as the second Adam, and because he applies all that work to those who believe, we also see in Revelation 21–22 the culmination of God's original intent for Adam and Eve to be fruitful and multiply. The description of the new creation is first of all a description of the new Israel, restored to the new Jerusalem and dwelling with God in his new temple. All God's promises to Israel find their yes in Christ, already in his earthly ministry and culminated here in the new cre-ation. Jesus, in his person the fulfillment of all God's promises to Israel, now applies that fulfillment to all the earth. But in doing so it is not only ethnic Jews who benefit, just as in this age it is not only ethnic Jews who benefit from Christ's saving work. This new Israel is the Israel of God, the true Israel made up of both Jew and Gentile.

God calls Israel out of the world for the sake of the world. God redeems the world through Israel. And we see the fulfillment of this in Revelation 21–22, when the new Israel is coterminous with the new creation. In renewing Israel, God renews the world. God in Christ is fruitful and multiplies by bringing in people from all tribes, tongues, and nations by the power of his Spirit and to the glory of the Father.

This is the vision that Revelation 21–22 gives us: that through the work of Jesus Christ in both his advents, God restores what Adam and Eve lost in the garden. Now, his redeemed image bearers can do what Adam and Eve did not: rule well in his place where they dwell with him, cultivating it and keeping it, and doing so throughout the whole cosmos because God has been fruitful and multiplied his people through the work of the Son by the power of the Holy Spirit. We wait for this now, between the times, so that we can say with John, "Maranatha! Come, Lord Jesus!"[11]

---

[11] On Revelation and the end of the story line, see T. Desmond Alexander, *From Eden to the New Jerusalem: An Introduction to Biblical Theology* (Grand Rapids: Kregel Academic, 2008); Goldsworthy, *According to Plan*, 226–36; and Roberts, *God's Big Picture*, 147–62.

CHAPTER 5

Exploring Biblical Terrains

Now that we've surveyed the big picture, there are a number of ways to explore the smaller areas of the map. We could, like some, work our way through the different major themes of Scripture. We could also, as others have done, work our way book by book or section by section through the Bible. Given our metaphor of the topographical map, my aim in this chapter is to demonstrate at least two themes that, along with the main story we've told, give the map a particular structure: covenant and kingdom. We can think of the big story of the Bible as the mountain peaks of ranges that run throughout, giving us landmarks along the way that help us to find our bearings and show us where we are going. These two themes of covenant and kingdom are the mountain ranges themselves, culminating in those peaks of the bigger story but always providing backbone to the terrain, whether through peaking in that big story or in the valleys and lower mountainous regions in between. In turn, these structural backbones also help us to describe those valleys and lower mountainous regions, what we might call, simply, "themes." So, we begin by describing the backbone themes of covenant and kingdom and then will show how other themes are connected to those.

Primary Themes

Covenant

As we saw in the previous three chapters, what moves the narrative along from Creation and Fall to Redemption and Restoration (or New Creation) are the different covenants God makes with his people in order to restore his kingdom.[1] This story moves in many ways along covenantal lines. God promises to redeem the world through Eve's seed, and this seed's coming is traced through those with whom God makes his covenants—Noah, Abraham, and David. Further, the covenants God makes are intended to reverse the curse of Adam. As we noted in the story line, God's original purposes for Adam—to dwell, rule, obey, cultivate, and multiply—are what God intends to restore through keeping his covenants, and what he does restore through the new covenant inaugurated by Israel's Messiah, Jesus. The theme of covenant, therefore, draws a line through the Old Testament material and points to the Old Testament's fulfillment in the new covenant, inaugurated in the person and work of Jesus. Covenants, thus, form the backbone of the biblical material.

Note that the previous paragraph does not mention the Sinaitic covenant. This is because that particular covenant both fits into and is different from the other three mentioned. The Sinaitic covenant is like the other covenants in that its promises are related to restoring

---

[1] On the twin themes of covenant and kingdom, and how they structure the biblical story, see Craig G. Bartholomew and Michael W. Goheen, *The Drama of Scripture: Finding Our Place in the Biblical Story* (Grand Rapids: Baker Academic, 2004), 25–27.

Adam's tasks and their culmination found in Christ. But it is unlike the other covenants in that it is temporally and ethnically limited. In other words, as Paul notes (cf. Gal 3:15–29, among others), it is only for the Jewish people before the Messiah comes, and it can be and is broken by the Jews to the point that God invokes its curse of exile on them. This is important for how we understand Jesus's work in inaugurating the new covenant: it is both continuous and discontinuous with the Sinaitic covenant. Jesus fulfills the Sinaitic law that Israel continually disobeyed. Jesus fulfills the promises of the Sinaitic covenant by defeating Israel's enemies and ruling over the promised land, but he does so in radically unexpected ways. In at least these two ways, Jesus's work is continuous with the Sinaitic covenant.

Jesus's work also is discontinuous with Israel's life under God's covenant with Moses. Instead of being only for ethnic Israel, the new covenant is for true Israel, all those who repent and believe. Instead of expecting ethnocentric and culturally conditioned laws to be obeyed, Jesus tells his followers to obey the new covenant law of the Spirit, the law of the created order that transcends ethnic and temporal boundaries. Instead of a temporary and conditional covenant, the new covenant is one in which its participants are sealed by the Spirit for the day of redemption (Eph 1:13–14). And instead of including only those who are physically descended from Abraham, the new covenant is for all who confess that Jesus is Lord and that God raised him from the dead. These are Abraham's children by faith, not by the flesh.

Thus, each of the Old Testament covenants—the Noahic, Abrahamic, Sinaitic, and Davidic—look forward to YHWH restoring what Adam lost, and they are thus joined together in the new covenant's inauguration in Christ. While we need to distinguish the temporally and ethnically limited Sinaitic covenant from the more universal nature of the others (especially the Noahic and Abraham-ic), it still contains God's promises to proleptically restore what Adam lost in the geopolitical nation of Israel, and thus points us forward to the other covenants' fulfillment for the sake of the whole world in the person and work of Jesus. In this way he fulfills, in the new covenant, both the Sinaitic covenant for the sake of geopolitical Israel and the Noahic, Abrahamic, and Davidic covenants for the sake of the world.[2]

Kingdom

The theme of kingdom is also structurally and thematically important for the Bible, and goes hand in hand with the structural theme of covenant. This is because the covenants are God's promises to restore the kingdom that was established and lost in the garden. When we say that the covenants are promises to "restore what Adam lost," we need to be clear that what Adam lost was not simply his and Eve's individual relationship with God (although that certainly was lost as well). What was lost was the kingdom that God had established through Adam and Eve and which he commanded them to expand. They were to rule over that garden kingdom in obedience, cultivating the land given to them and expanding its borders. So, when God makes promises to Noah, Abraham, and David to restore what Adam lost, he is promising to restore his kingdom.

Further, the promises he makes show us how he will restore that kingdom and what it will look like. So, with God's promise to Noah, we see that God's kingdom will be a restoration of the entire cosmos through the judgment of sin. In the promise to Abraham, we see that God's kingdom involves his people whom he creates dwelling

---

[2]   See, for instance, N. T. Wright, *The Climax of the Covenant: Christ and the Law in Pauline Theology* (Minneapolis: Fortress, 1992), 18–40.

with him in, cultivating, and expanding the borders of a land that he gives to them, all while obeying his law. Then with David, God's kingdom is shown to be a place where David's Son rules forever and builds God's temple. And even though the Mosaic covenant is conditional and temporal, in it and in the life of Israel in the land we see a prefigurement of what God's global kingdom will look like when he comes on the day of the Lord to establish it. Additionally, in each of these promises we are reminded of the fundamental promise that God made to Adam and Eve in the garden, the promise related to how God would reestablish his kingdom—through the Seed of woman, which we later learn to call the Messiah, or God's Servant.

Both of these structural backbones need to inform how we understand what Jesus is doing in the Gospels. It is not a throwaway phrase that Jesus, Matthew, and Mark use when they refer to the "gospel of the kingdom of God" (Matt 4:23; 9:35; 24:14; Mark 1:15). Jesus's life and work is not just good news because it restores individual sinners' souls to God (although that certainly is good news!). It is good news because it is the good news of the kingdom, the good news that, through Jesus, YHWH has restored his kingdom that was lost in the fall and prefigured in Israel. Jesus's kingdom, which encompasses the entire cosmos, cannot and will not be lost. As we saw in chapter 4, Jesus fulfills all the promises to Noah, Abraham, Moses, and David and, in doing so, restores all that Adam and Eve lost—namely, God's kingdom. Thus, covenant and kingdom go hand in hand: they are about restoring what Adam and Eve lost, *and* they are fulfilled in the person and work of Jesus.[3]

---

[3] On the relationship between kingdom and covenant, see Bartholomew and Goheen, *The Drama of Scripture*, 25–27.

Additional Themes

We could trace a multitude of themes throughout Scripture or within different parts of Scripture, and other biblical theological texts have attempted to do so. For instance, we could work through biblical texts related to the theme of temple or of kingship or of sacrifice. We could discuss the people of God or justification. All of these projects would be beneficial. Here, though, I only wish to trace a few themes and, specifically, ones that obviously relate to and help us to further clarify the structural backbones of covenant and kingdom.

Creation and Wisdom

Perhaps the easiest starting point for discussion of themes that tie together covenant and kingdom is to talk about creation and wisdom. These twin themes are found throughout the Old Testament, and they are foundational to biblical theology and to the biblical story. A term that ties these two terms together is "created order."[4] God makes the world to work in a certain way. There is an order to the cosmos. This includes everything from "natural laws" like gravity to the rotation of the planets to the ways that different kinds of creatures relate to one another to how creatures of the same kind relate to one another (i.e., male and female human beings). Order is a reference, therefore, to the way the creation operates under God's initial creative act and his ongoing sustaining work.

There is, however, another aspect to this order, an aspect that is unique to those who bear his image, human beings. Humans, given the ability by God to choose obedience or disobedience, are expected to live wisely within this created order. That is, unlike the rest

---

[4] See Albert M. Wolters, *Creation Regained: Biblical Basics for a Reformational Worldview*, 2nd ed. (Grand Rapids: Eerdmans, 2005), 14.

of creation (other than the angels), human beings uniquely share in the ability to participate in the created order as rational creatures. They make decisions related to God's command to them. There are only two options in this regard: obedience and disobedience. The Old Testament refers to these two choices, respectively, as wisdom and folly. For rational, image-bearing creatures, the choice before us is always wisdom or folly, obedience or disobedience. Adam and Eve, the first image bearers, chose folly through disobedience and cast the rest of their descendants into the resulting fallen state of all creation. We are all, therefore, subsequently prone to wander, prone to seek out Lady Folly instead of Lady Wisdom (see Proverbs 1–9), prone to seek death instead of life. While the Old Testament repeatedly calls its hearers to wisdom through obedience, it also continually describes Israel and the nations as unable to obey. Jesus converges these two threads by doing what Israel cannot. He is the Wisdom of God (1 Cor 1:24) and, as the Spirit-anointed Messiah, the One who obeys on Israel's behalf. He is the embodiment of the created order and the image-bearing responsibility to live wisely in it—and, therefore, also the fulfillment of what Israel and the nations cannot do in the Old Testament, wisely obey God's Word. So, the biblical story line points forward to a time when God's created order will be restored from the effects of Adam's fall through God's Servant.

God's Servant

The theme of God's Servant[5] also ties together covenant and kingdom. Throughout the Old Testament we see God working through priests, prophets, and kings to restore his people to himself.

---

[5] See Stephen G. Dempster, "The Servant of the Lord," 128–78 in *Central Themes in Biblical Theology: Mapping Unity in Diversity*, ed. Scott J. Hafemann and Paul R. House (Grand Rapids: Baker Academic, 2007).

Each of these three offices is an important piece of what God's Spirit-anointed messianic Servant will be. With respect to the first, in the Old Testament God's prophets faithfully declare his Spirit-given Word, denouncing sin and calling for repentance and faith. His priests make sacrifices so that his people can draw close to him in his temple. And his kings rule over his place, ideally in faithfulness to God and leading the people in obedience, so that God's people can care for his place and expand its borders (e.g., David in 2 Samuel 5–10). God's Servant, the coming Messiah who will restore what Adam lost, is spoken of in each of these terms.[6] Further, God's Servant will not just offer a sacrifice but will be the atoning sacrifice, the One who pays for the sins of his people with his own life (see the Suffering Servant songs in Isaiah 42–54). The covenants are fulfilled through this Spirit-anointed Servant, Jesus, who declares God's Word faithfully and calls on people to repent and believe, who offers himself as the sacrifice for the sins of his people, and who, having obeyed in every respect, now rules over the world, cultivating his kingdom and multiplying his people through his Spirit.

Mission

This brings us to the third theme that runs throughout the Bible's covenant-kingdom structure: mission.[7] God makes the world in such a way that his people are put in his place and then expected to expand it. But after Adam and Eve fail to obey the Lord, God goes on a redemptive mission to restore what was lost and bring a broken world back to himself (see Col 1:16–20). He is now on a global mission to redeem his fallen creation, the entire cosmos, through his

---

[6] On these various roles of God's Servant, see ibid., esp. 164–65, 177–78.

[7] On this theme see Michael W. Goheen, *A Light to the Nations: The Missional Church and the Biblical Story* (Grand Rapids: Baker Academic, 2011).

people Israel. And God expected Adam and Eve to participate with him in advancing his creational mission, as he also expected Israel and now the church to participate with him in his global redemptive mission. Israel, in a way that foreshadows Jesus and his church, is to be a light to the nations, a royal priesthood, a holy nation. And when the fulfillment of Israel's hope, Jesus—the true Israel—comes, he is now the one who draws the world to himself through his Spirit.

And it is not only the God-Man and his Spirit at work; it is God at work through Christ by the power of his Spirit in his church. The church is Christ's body, united to him by faith and the Spirit's transforming power, and as his body they participate with him in his mission. They are called to be his ambassadors (2 Cor 5:17), spreading the good news of Christ's kingship to those near and far. They are now the royal priesthood and holy nation that Israel was supposed to be but never was and, thus, are to "declare the praises of him who called you out of darkness into his wonderful light" (1 Pet 2:10). They are little Adams and Eves, created through Jesus breathing his Spirit on them (John 20:21; cf. Gen 2:7), now called to be fruitful and multiply through sharing the good news of Christ's victorious work of salvation in his death and resurrection "in Jerusalem, in Judea and Samaria, and to the ends of the earth" (Acts 1:8).

Salvation through Faith

This brings us to a final (at least for our purposes) theme that is threaded throughout the covenant-kingdom backbone of the Bible: salvation through faith. Those who are part of the new covenant participate in it through repentance and belief. Members of the new covenant community are truly redeemed from their sin, forgiven through Jesus's work of atonement in his death and resurrection, and trust not in their own works to save them but in Christ's work alone. We call this radical trust in Christ and not in ourselves "faith." And the term we usually use to refer to what happens when a person has faith is "justification." That is, when someone trusts in Christ's work to save him, he trusts that Christ's death and resurrection justifies him before God. Previously an enemy of God because of his sin, the one who has faith is now justified, made right, before God through his faith in Christ's work (e.g., Rom 3:21–26).

We see over and over again throughout Scripture that God calls people to repent—turn from—their sins and believe in his ability and his alone to save them. He calls Abram out of Ur of the Chaldeans, and Abram responds in faith. He makes a covenant with Abram, and Abram believes—has faith, trusts—and this is credited to him as righteousness (Gen 15:6). He's justified, saved, made right with God through faith in God's work, not his own. God calls Israel out of Egypt, and they are expected to respond in faith. Some do, and are made right before God, but most do not (e.g., Judg 2:11–15). The prophets, before, during, and after the exile, call Israel and the nations to turn from their sin in repentance and turn to God, who alone can save them (e.g., Joel 2:18–32). And this is the same call Jesus makes in the Gospels. Turn from your sin, repent, and turn to Christ whose work alone can save you (e.g., Mark 1:14–15). This is now the call that God makes to the nations through his church, his global ambassadors (2 Cor 5:17). We proclaim the good news that Christ, the God-Man, has accomplished salvation through his life, death, resurrection, ascension, and gift of the Spirit and now rules and reigns forever.

In proclaiming this gospel, the only gospel, God through his Spirit calls people to repent and believe. Those who respond in faith are saved, experiencing eternal life now with God and hoping for the day when he returns in glory (Rom 8:1–30). Those who do not respond in faith, if they continue to reject God's appeal in Christ through us, will perish and spend eternity separated from God. The day of the Lord has come in Christ, but it is coming again when he returns. That day, spread across Christ's two advents, separates in judgment those who respond in faith to YHWH's work in Christ and those who respond in obstinacy. The former group experiences eternal life with God on the new heavens and new earth; the latter group experiences eternal death, separated from God, in the lake of fire (Rev 21:1–8). So, this appeal that we make as the church, as ambassadors of Christ, is urgent. God calls us through his Spirit, sent by Christ, and expects a response.

Tying It All Together

As is hopefully evident by now, all of these themes are intricately connected. The big story of the Bible—Creation, Fall, Redemption, New Creation—has as its backbone the twin themes of covenant and kingdom. These themes, in turn, are further clarified by the themes of creation and wisdom, God's Servant, mission, and call and response. These latter, smaller themes are how the covenant is fulfilled and how the kingdom is inaugurated and expanded. In turn, the themes of covenant and kingdom help us to see how God restores his creation.

As we move from "smaller themes" to "backbone themes" to "overarching story" then, what we are seeing is how each of these smaller layers is the means by which the next layer up is accomplished. God moves from creation to new creation through covenant and kingdom, and in turn covenant and kingdom are enacted through creation and wisdom, God's Servant, mission, and call and response. The Bible, as we've said, is an intricate web, both textually and thematically, and we need to see the whole in order to understand the parts and vice versa. These themes and their interconnectivity help us to do just that.

CHAPTER 6

Using the Map: Practical Applications for Biblical Theology

N ow that we've explored the biblical terrain, what help does this give us in the Christian life? As with any map, understanding the topographical terrain of the Bible can assist us in getting to any number of places. Of course, ultimately, the main trail leads to seeing and knowing Jesus Christ. But we can take any number of side trails, each of which, while distinct, help us along that main Christological path.

In this chapter we will explore how biblical theology can be put to practical use in our preaching, doctrinal formulation, pastoral counseling, and living the Christian life (I will focus upon our devotional exercises and our mission). In short, biblical theology is crucial for knowing where we are, where we are going, and how to get from point A to point B. This is true not only for the main purpose of the Bible, to know God in the face of Jesus Christ through the power of the Spirit, but also for each of the auxiliary and derivative purposes for Scripture.

Preaching and Teaching

Because I focused on expository preaching in my master's degree courses, the proclamation of God's Word typically comes to mind first when I think about applying any particular concept. It is difficult for me to overstate the importance of biblical theology for the preacher's task. In virtually every hermeneutics class or textbook I've heard of, the teacher or author rightly emphasizes the context of the passage. To understand a text appropriately, the preacher or teacher must understand its context, where it is located, which paragraph or section of the biblical book. Biblical theology helps locate the passage not only in its immediate context but also in its canonical context.

If we think about Scripture like a vast web, every thread leads to other threads and is part of the whole web. Biblical theology helps us to see how our particular point in the web (text) is connected to other parts of the web (canonical context) and contributes to the making of the whole web (biblical story). Or, to use our map analogy, immediate context shows us where we are on one particular side trail, but biblical theology helps us to see how that particular side trail connects to the larger pathways that lead to the main trail. At the risk of using one too many illustrations in a biblical theology sermon, we can also think about Charles Spurgeon's well-known instruction to preachers: "make a beeline to the cross." Biblical theology helps us to see how the different webs or trails connect so we can get from our particular text to the cross of Christ, without running roughshod over the rest of the terrain to get there.

The two main tools we can use to do this are typology and intertextuality. Sometimes a particular text fits into a larger pattern of texts that repeat stories or have commonalities between the people in the story. As we noted in the introduction, this typological shape of Scripture can be followed from its beginning in Genesis to its end in Christ. This way of seeing the entirety of Scripture as one big book with one big theme allows us to note how a particular text fits into one or more of these major patterns, or types.

The second tool that we've also already discussed in the introduction is intertextuality. Here the analogies of the web and the side trails connecting through pathways to the main trail again come into play. When we notice that a particular text is connected to some other text, it is many times through that connection also connecting to the main pathway of Scripture. Like streams connect to tributaries and tributaries connect to the main river, intertextuality helps us to see that individual passages connect to bigger textual tributaries through Scripture, which then connect us to the main Christological river. All of this is to say that biblical theology helps us to see the "big picture" of Scripture and how a particular passage fits into that. In doing so, our sermons and teaching outlines become more robust, more intricately connected to what God is saying in the whole Bible.

Doctrine

If we recognize the canonical context of biblical passages in our preaching and teaching, we ought to do so in our theological reflection as well. As we seek to understand God's revelation systematically, we cannot do so through simply pointing to individual texts divorced from their immediate and canonical contexts. Proof-texting, while easy, doesn't situate us on the map properly. Biblical theology seeks to ensure that, when we ask what the Bible says about a particular theological topic, our answer gives appropriate consideration to the biblical terrain. So, for instance, when we talk about the doctrine of salvation, attention must be given not only to how individual people come to know God in Christ—as vital as that is!—but also to the holistic purpose God has for what he does through Christ. That holistic purpose includes saving individual sinners who repent and believe in Christ's work, to be sure—as our tour of the biblical story showed—but the salvation of individual image bearers is couched within God's larger purpose, to restore all that Adam and Eve lost by fulfilling his covenant with Abraham. That larger purpose places the salvation of individuals in the communal context of restoring God's people, the cosmological context of renewing God's place, and the covenantal context of rescuing his image bearers from sin and renewing their spirits. In other words, salvation is not only about individuals getting a "get out of hell free" card but about God saving his entire creation, with humanity at its head. This kind of attention to the shape of the biblical story ought to be given to every doctrine, whether salvation or creation or morality.

Counseling

Speaking of morality, biblical theology can be of great assistance in pastoral counseling. I teach undergraduate students, and often their main question is vocational—what does God want me to do with my life? Biblical theology, in demonstrating the big picture of the Bible, assists us in situating our lives within that bigger story. Instead of our story being the main play, we see that we're all merely supposed to see how our story fits into God's bigger story, the story of his redemption of the whole world (more about this mission below).

Biblical theology also assists us in answering ethical questions, such as ones regarding the value of human life or sexuality. When a member of your youth group comes and asks for a specific verse forbidding abortion or sex before marriage, there are a few options but no real "slam dunk" proof-texts. We can show them another means of answering questions biblically, though, through biblical theology.

The shape of the biblical story regarding life shows us that God is the maker of all creatures, murder (the unjust taking of a life) is sinful, and humans in the womb are considered partakers with us in this creaturely, God-given life. Likewise regarding sexuality we see that sex is given in the context of marriage in Genesis 1–2, is a covenantal act both in the beginning and through the rest of the biblical story, and is a creational good that points beyond itself to the ultimate good of the marriage between Christ and his church (e.g., Eph 5:32).

The Christian Life

Devotion

One of the most common obstacles in the average Christian's devotional life, at least from what I can tell from conversations with fellow Christians, is that many don't know what they're supposed to be reading *for* when they read their Bibles. In other words, the Christians with whom I've talked will express discouragement about their Bible reading because they often are confused about the point of particular passages or books. Biblical theology helps here because its purpose is to help us see the big picture and how all the smaller plots fit into that one main story.

If you're a minister, you may not want to lead off with Irenaeus's talk of hypothesis, economy, and recapitulation, but you can certainly use biblical theology to help them see what Irenaeus was trying to show his readers: that the Bible has one main point, Jesus; that the Bible has one main story, which we've summarized as Creation, Fall, Redemption, and New Creation; and that the Bible is full of smaller stories that all point to the one main story of God the Son taking on human flesh and living, dying, rising, ascending, giving his Spirit, and promising to return in glory. This can assist the average Bible reader tremendously because they now have a framework for reading individual stories. We read individual stories in light of the bigger story about Jesus and, therefore, ask how that smaller story connects, whether through intertextuality or typology, to that bigger story.

Another important aspect of pointing Bible readers to Jesus as the main point of Scripture is that it is through seeing Jesus that we are transformed into his image. Paul tells us in 2 Cor 3:17–18 that as we see Jesus, we are made to be more like him by his Spirit. Knowing God in Christ and being transformed into Christ's image by his Spirit is the point of the Christian life. Biblical theology gives us the framework to know God by seeing Christ in his Spirit-inspired Word, which in turn is used by the Spirit to make us more like Jesus.

Mission

Biblical theology also gives us the outward aim of the Christian life, to be on mission for God. We are called in many passages to share the good news of Jesus Christ, whether it be in the Gospels when Jesus tells us that we are the light of the world and a city on a hill (Matt 5:14), or in the Letters, as in 2 Cor 5:17, where Paul calls us ambassadors for Christ. Biblical theology gives these texts a larger context and helps us to see they are at the heart of God's intent for his church. The church is a church on mission because God's intention for his image bearers is to be fruitful and multiply and fill all the earth with other worshippers of YHWH. Mission—whether it be international missions, evangelism, discipleship, or love in action in our community—is not just one part of the Christian life; it is the purpose for the Christian life in this age between the times of Christ's first and second advents. While our first and ultimate purpose is to love the LORD our God with all our heart, soul, mind, and strength, this inward devotion is never divorced from the second and derivative purpose, to love our neighbor as ourselves. We love our neighbors by discipling them into the image of Christ. Mission is about disciple making. The big picture of the Bible, therefore, helps us to see that our Christian life is not compartmentalized into church attendance, church service, missions, evangelism, discipleship, and the like; it is a holistic exercise in participating in God's mission to the nations.

Conclusion

Biblical theology is inherently practical because the Bible is inherently practical. The Bible is not only for information but also for transformation. Further, these two go hand in hand. As we understand better how to read Scripture, we understand its message better and, therefore, are better able to be transformed by it. Biblical theology gives us the framework to read Scripture. Yes, other tools are needed, but without this big picture, without our topographical map, it's easy to lose our place in the forest because we are so busy looking at individual trees. Biblical theology helps us to see where we are in the forest and to make our way toward the end of our trail, the end of all biblical trails, the person and work of Jesus. As we strive toward that end, biblical theology tells us which turns we need to take to stay on that main Christological path. In doing so, it orients our devotion, mission, doctrine, counseling, and preaching and teaching toward that same goal.

Name and Subject Index

Scripture Index

CPSIA information can be obtained
at www.ICGtesting.com
Printed in the USA
LVOW10*1105240118
563579LV00004B/32/P